Reinvent the Wheel

Reinvent the Wheel

Make Classic Inventions,
Discover Your Problem-Solving Genius,
and Take the Inventor's Challenge

RUTH KASSINGER

John Wiley & Sons, Inc.

New York • Chichester • Weinheim • Brisbane • Singapore • Toronto

Published by John Wiley & Sons, Inc.
Published simultaneously in Canada

Design and production by Navta Associates, Inc.

The publisher and the author have made every reasonable effort to ensure that the experiments and activities in the book are safe when conducted as instructed but assume no responsibility for any damage caused or sustained while performing the experiments or activities in this book. Parents, guardians, and/or teachers should supervise young readers who undertake the experiments and activities in this book.

Designations used by companies to distinguish their products are often claimed as trademarks. In all instances where John Wiley & Sons, Inc., is aware of a claim, the product names appear in Initial Capital or ALL CAPITAL letters. Readers, however, should contact the appropriate companies for more complete information regarding trademarks and registration.

Library of Congress Cataloging-in-Publication Data:

Kassinger, Ruth
    Reinvent the wheel : make classic inventions, discover your problem-solving genius, and take the inventor's challenge / Ruth Kassinger.
       p. cm.
    Includes index.
     ISBN 0-471-39539-0
     1. Inventions–Juvenile literature.   2. Inventions–History–Juvenile literature.
    [1. Inventions.]   I. Title.
     T212 .K37   2001
     608–dc21   2001000109

Printed in the United States of America

10 9 8 7 6 5 4 3 2 1

Contents

To Ellen Roberts

Acknowledgments

I am grateful for the continuing assistance of Dr. Burton Edelson, James Polk, and Bruce Higley in matters of science and engineering. I also owe thanks to my homegrown inventors, Anna, Austen, Alice, and their friends who helped with the experiments in this book; to Ted Kassinger for his good-humored and unstinting support; and to Kate Bradford for her deft editing.

Introduction

Imagine a world without wheels. There'd be no cars, of course, and no bicycles, skateboards, roller blades, or scooters. Imagine a world without paints and dyes. All your clothes would be white, beige, brown, gray, and black because those are the colors of sheep's wool, goat's hair, llama fur, and fabric made of cotton and other plants. The walls and floors of your house would be the earth tones of stone, mud, brick, or wood.

We take for granted wheels and paints, as well as thermometers, compasses, batteries, and many other everyday things. At one time, though, these things were brand-new. Someone somewhere invented them. Who invented them, and how? And how can you become an inventor, too?

This book answers those questions. We'll never know exactly who first came up with most of the ancient inventions. Why not? Because many were invented before people invented writing (about 5000 B.C.), so no one could write down the names of the inventors! Even so, we can figure out *how* inventors made their inventions, and we can imagine *why* they did. For the more recent inventions, we can read the inventors' own descriptions and look at their drawings.

In a world without wheels, there would be no doorknobs. There would be no doors either! What do wheels have to do with doors? Take a close look at how a door joins the wall. The metal hinges are axles around which a circular sleeve turns. A door hinge is actually a wheel and axle!

Imagine that you don't know how to hit a baseball, but you want to learn how to do it. You could try to learn by reading about how to do it. If you really want to learn how it's done, though, you need to try it yourself. You need to experiment. How soon should you start to swing? Should you step toward the ball? Is it better to hold the bat near the bottom of the handle or up higher?

In the same way, the best way to figure out how people invented things is to try to invent them yourself. This book explains the problems inventors faced, which inspired them to invent. It tells you what materials they used. Then, just like the original inventors, you will create a problem-solving invention. Sometimes you'll make a full-size invention; sometimes you'll make a working model.

How do inventors go about inventing? In movies and cartoons, mad scientists and eccentric inventors work in gloomy basements hammering together odds and ends, trying to give shape to a wild idea that exists in

Of course, you will have a few advantages that the original inventors didn't have. This book gives you lots of practical suggestions to help you on your way. It explains some science that our ancestors didn't understand, which will make your inventing easier. You'll also find the story of how past inventors really did come up with their inventions, so you can learn from their experience. Also, finally, at the end of each chapter, you'll face a challenge: to solve a problem with an invention of your own.

their imagination. At last, they emerge from the gloom with a peculiar, clanking invention that sort of works and isn't actually very useful. Is that how inventing is done? Sorry, Mr. Disney, but no.

Inventions often get started because an ordinary someone is irritated. This ordinary someone is so fed up with a practical problem that he or she becomes inspired to solve it with an invention. In this book you'll see, for example, that prehistoric artists could have been motivated to invent paints because they were annoyed that people accidentally smeared their chalk and charcoal cave-wall drawings.

Other inventions are the by-products of scientific investigation. Alessandro Volta, for example, didn't imagine a battery and then set out to invent it. His friend Luigi Galvani had discovered that the legs of a dead frog would twitch when touched by metals. Volta was troubled by Galvani's explanation—that animals contained electricity even when dead—and set out to find what really caused the twitching. The end result was the wet-cell battery.

Some inventors are driven by a desire to make the world a better place. For example, in the 1940s, Buckminster Fuller set himself a goal of creating cheap, easy-to-build houses that could be dropped from an airplane wherever they were needed. With this goal in mind, he experimented with buildings made from plastic triangles and invented the geodesic dome.

All inventors are good observers. They take inspiration from the world around them and adapt both natural and synthetic (made by humans) things to make their new inventions. In about 1450, for example, Johannes Gutenberg was looking for a way to press paper against type for his invention, the printing press. To make it, he adapted the design of the wine press, a device people had been using for thousands of years to squeeze juice out of grapes.

Some inventions are pure accident. In 1856, William Henry Perkin accidentally invented synthetic dyes when trying to produce *quinine*, a medicine to treat malaria, out of coal tars. He noticed that one of his failures—a black, sticky goo—produced a beautiful, light purple color when mixed in water.

Even accidental inventors, though, have to have good imaginations. How many of us would have thrown away the black goo in disgust? It took a curious attitude and imagination to discover a beautiful dye in a sticky mess.

Inventions don't usually arrive in an inventor's brain in perfect form. Inventors have an idea and then they experiment. They try it this way and then that way. They add a little of this and then a little of that. They try it upside up and then upside down. Michael Faraday was convinced that magnetism could create electricity. He experimented for years with different arrangements of magnets and copper wire before he found one that produced electrical current.

The last step for inventors is to give their invention to the world. The invention may solve the inventor's problem and answer the inventor's question, but will other people like it and use it? Some inventions take off; some don't.

In the 1890s, a man named J. C. Boyle was irritated by having to reach up and tip his hat in greeting to ladies (as was the custom of the time). So, he invented a "saluting device" that automatically tipped his hat. A patent for the device was issued on March 10, 1896. It seems, though, that most men didn't find that tipping a hat was a big burden. Mr. Boyle's device never caught on.

All the inventions in this book caught on, though. People have used compasses for at least 1,100 years. They've used mechanical fans for more than 2,000 years and wheels for nearly 5,500 years. Some of the paints that you find in your classroom and at home today were invented by prehistoric artists more than 20,000 years ago! Most of the inventions in this book have been so successful, it's hard to imagine the world without them.

PART I

Inventions Based on Simple Machines

Think of a machine. What pops into your head? You might have thought of tractors, washing machines, motorcycles, drills, or computers. You probably didn't think of an inclined plane (which looks like a ramp), a wedge, a screw, a lever, a pulley, or a wheel and axle. These are the most basic machines, called the **simple machines**. They are the building blocks for many, more complex machines.

Machines make work easier. It is easier to lift a bucket of cement with a pulley than to hoist it with your arms alone. It is easier to move a boulder on a cart with wheels than to drag the boulder across the ground. Most machines make work easier because they multiply the effort you put into the machine.

Several million years ago, members of an early human species must have invented the first lever to dig up edible roots. Early human beings must have also discovered it was easier to walk up a sloping tree trunk that had conveniently fallen in front of the entrance to their hillside cave rather than climbing straight up. They invented a machine—the inclined plane—when, at another cave, they purposely placed a trunk or a few branches to make an entrance ramp.

The wedge is nearly as ancient. About 2 million years ago, people began to use a pointed stone to chip away at the edges of another stone to form a sharp scraping tool. They were using the first stone as a wedge to split flakes of stone off their scraper.

The wheel, the screw, and the pulley are much more recent inventions, within the past 5,000 years. Although tools that rely on inclined planes, wedges, and levers are universal, not all cultures developed wheels, screws, and pulleys. In Part I of this book, you'll learn about some inventions based on simple machines. When you finish, try using what you've learned to make a new invention to help you spend less effort to do something.

1 Potter's Wheel

The Problem

You're a *potter* (someone who makes pots out of clay) somewhere in the ancient Middle East. You form your clay pots on a large, flat stone that lies on the ground. To make a pot smooth and uniform on all sides, you need to work on all sides of a pot. To work on all sides, however, you must constantly move around the pot, which is tiring and time-consuming. You would like to lift and turn the pot, but the clay is too soft. The pot would sag in your hands.

If you could just turn the slab instead. . . . How can you make the slab turn?

Observations

One day, when the afternoon sun is scorching, you drag your stone slab to a shady spot under a tree. A large pebble gets caught underneath the stone slab. You discover that the stone slab turns easily on top of the pebble.

MATERIALS

corrugated cardboard
carpet
drawing compass
pencil
scissors
posterboard
tape
plastic tape dispenser

Experiment

1. Cut the corrugated cardboard into two 9- × 12-inch (23-cm × 30-cm) rectangles.

2. Take one of the rectangles (this is your stone slab), and put it on a carpet. Try to spin it.

The problem here is friction. **Friction** is the resistance between two objects when they are pushed or pulled across one another. Friction stops the cardboard from spinning smoothly on the carpet. Friction also prevents a potter from spinning a stone slab when it lies flat against the ground.

3. Use the drawing compass to draw two 3-inch (8-cm) diameter circles on the posterboard. Cut out the circles.

4. Take one of the paper circles and cut a slit halfway across. Slide one slit edge under the other to make a cone shape. Tape the paper so it keeps its cone shape. Tape the cone to the table. Balance the rectangle on top of the cone, and then spin it.

The paper cone that you made is a pivot. A **pivot** is an object on which, or around which, another object turns. A pivot reduces the amount of friction between the turning object and the surface beneath it, so that the turning object can move more freely.

Between the top two vertebrae in your neck is a pivot joint that lets you turn your head. Scissors have a pivot that allows you to open and close the blades. The cone pivot in your experiment works like the pebble caught under the potter's slab.

5. Did you have a problem with your pivot and cardboard? Did the cardboard slip off? Take the scissors and make a small hole near the center of the cardboard. Now spin the cardboard.

The hole you just made in the cardboard is called a socket. A **socket** is an opening or hollow that forms a holder for something else. A socket helps keep the turning object in one place. Your own body has sockets: The top of each arm swivels in the socket of each shoulder bone.

6. Make another cone from the second paper circle. Tape the edges together, as before, and tape the cone to the center of the other piece of cardboard. Put the plastic tape dispenser flat on its side on the table. Stick the pivot into the hole in the dispenser, as shown. Now spin the cardboard. Which of your two spinning devices works better?

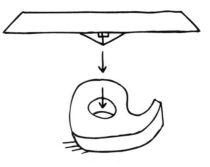

7. Is a rectangle the best shape for spinning? Could the pointed corners be a little dangerous to a potter sitting next to the wheel? How about balancing a rectangle—kind of hard? Would a circle be better? Trim your rectangle to a circle shape, and stick the pivot back into the socket of the tape dispenser. Now spin the cardboard in the tape dispenser again. You've done it: You've reinvented the potter's wheel!

Answers from the Past

In about 11,000 B.C. in Japan and about 8000 B.C. in the Middle East, people figured out how to shape clay pots and heat them in a fire until they became hard, waterproof, and flameproof. For many thousands of years, people formed their pots by pinching the clay or by coiling long clay ropes into a pot shape. To make the pots smooth and uniform all around, though, the potter had to move around the pot. Village potters making many pots would have been inspired to invent a way to turn the pots instead of turning themselves.

Many **archaeologists** (people who study ancient human fossils and tools) believe that people first invented the potter's wheel around 3500 B.C.—probably even before they invented the wheel for a vehicle! A pebble caught under a stone slab could well have been the inventor's inspiration. Early potter's wheels were made of stone or slabs of hardened clay, and potters turned them by hand. The potter's wheel was invented separately in China and in the Middle East at about the same time.

This invention spread all over the world. People discovered (just as you did) that they could either attach the pivot directly to the wheel or attach the pivot to a surface underneath. They found, as you did, that a pivot works best when it fits into a socket.

Potters also soon discovered that when they spun the wheel fast, their job of forming pots became easier in another way. When they spun the wheel fast, they could use a steady, gentle pressure from their fingers to shape the clay. Instead of having to push the clay in and out, the motion of the wheel did most of the work.

Potters could make pots more quickly when they used a rapidly spinning potter's wheel. The pots were also more uniform in shape and could have thinner walls. Such pots were less likely to break in the heat of the kiln, a special high-temperature oven for hardening pottery.

Potters today still use the potter's wheel. Modern potter's wheels are usually powered by electric motors. An electric potter's wheel keeps the wheel going at a steady rate, so the potter doesn't have to keep pushing the wheel with a hand or foot.

INVENTOR'S CHALLENGE

The wheel you made is still wobbly. Can you make a more stable platform for your "stone slab"?

Materials

another 9- × 12-inch (23-cm × 30-cm) piece of cardboard
a bunch of marbles
two lids from a jar or other container, one slightly smaller than the other
modeling clay

CLUE

Fit the lids and marbles together to turn your "stone slab."

Watch a modern potter start to make a pot on a potter's wheel, and you'll see that the potter throws the clay hard onto the center of the wheel. Why? Everything moving in a circle experiences centrifugal force. **Centrifugal force** causes objects moving in a circle to move outward from the center of the circle. (If you've looked into a washing machine during its spin cycle, you have seen how centrifugal force flings the clothes outward, squeezing them against the side of the basket.) The potter slams the clay onto the wheel to make it stick better so that centrifugal force won't throw the pot across the room!

2 Vehicle Wheel

The Problem

You are a farmer outside the city of Ur in the ancient empire of Mesopotamia about 3500 B.C. Every morning, you harness your old goat to a **travois** (pronounced "trav-wah"), which is made of two long poles holding a wide leather sling attached between the lower halves of the poles. The lower tips of the poles rest on the ground. You tie the upper ends of the poles to your goat. You put your pottery jugs filled with goat's milk in the sling and lead your goat to the market.

You know the load is heavy. As your goat pulls the travois, the tips of the poles on the ground make long gouges in the earth. It's slow going, and the goat struggles to pull the load. There must be an easier way to get the milk to the market.

Observations

Frequently, you stop by the potter's house to trade for new jugs to store your milk. You watch the potter turn her pots on a flat stone wheel. Watching her spin the wheel, you get an idea. . . .

MATERIALS

cardboard box 1 foot (30 cm) wide or less, such as a shoe box

two 3-foot- (90-cm) long dowels about ⅜ inch (1 cm) in diameter

glue

two 18-inch (45-cm) dowels about ⅜ inch (1 cm) in diameter

string

plate, lid, or other circular object about 8 inches (20 cm) in diameter

corrugated cardboard

pencil

scissors

Experiment

1. First, make a travois. Glue the 18-inch (45-cm) dowels to the underside of the cardboard box. The dowels should be close to two opposite edges of the box. Leave at least 3 inches (7.5 cm) of each dowel overhanging either side of the box.

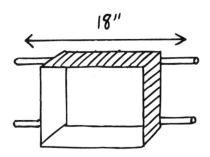

2. Put the remaining two dowels parallel to each other on the ground. Place the box on top of the long dowels so that the short dowels are perpendicular to them. The box should be about 2 inches (5 cm) from the end of the long dowels.

3. Use the string to lash the perpendicular dowels together so that the box is secured to the long dowels. (Wrap your string around the dowels in an "X" pattern.) This is your travois. Try pulling it around behind you on a rough surface (such as a carpet). Try it with a heavy book in the box.

4. Using the plate, lid, or other circular object roughly 8 inches (20 cm) in diameter, trace four circles on the corrugated cardboard. Cut out the circles. Glue two together, then glue the other two circles together, so you have two wheels, each made of two layers of cardboard.

5. Using your scissors, carefully make a hole in the center of each wheel. Each hole should be just a bit bigger than the dowels.

6. Slip the wheels onto the ends of the lower dowels that are sticking out from the box.

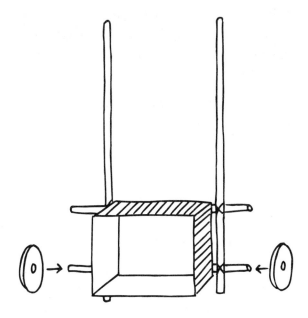

7. Now pull your copy of the world's first wheeled vehicle! Is it easier to pull than the travois?

Answers from the Past

The world's first vehicle wheels were invented in Mesopotamia (part of modern Iraq) about 3500 B.C. It is not easy to precisely date objects from so long ago, but it seems that vehicle wheels were invented just after the potter's wheel. A potter's wheel may well have inspired a farmer with a travois. Still, it took quite a leap of imagination to see how a flat wheel would be useful in moving heavy objects!

The first wheels were made from a slice of a thick tree branch or trunk. Holes were gouged in the middle of the wheels, and the wheels were slipped onto a pole called an **axle** (a bar on which one or more wheels turn). The early wheels spun around a *fixed* (immovable) axle, just as the wheels on your travois spin around a fixed dowel. Later, people attached the wheel to the axle, and the wheel and axle turned together.

Many cars and trucks today are "rear-wheel-drive" cars. In rear-wheel-drive cars, the power of the engine is transmitted to the rear axle, and the wheels are attached to the axle. Why are the wheels attached? It's important that the right and left wheels on the power axle spin at exactly the same rate. If they spun at even slightly different speeds, your car would go in circles.

The idea of wheels spread from Mesopotamia throughout Europe. Wheels made out of a solid piece of tree trunk or branch were largely abandoned because the wood split too easily under the weight of a load. Soon, people discovered how to make wheels by attaching three pieces of wood to each other side by side and then cutting the wood into a circle. Later, to keep the wheel rim from wearing down, people attached a strip of copper to it (the first tire!) or hammered lots of nails into it.

Although wheels made of three pieces of wood were sturdy, they were also very heavy. They added to the weight that the animal pulling the vehicle had to haul. People discovered that one way to reduce the weight of a wheel was to carve holes in it. Over time, they carved larger and larger holes. In time, the wheels came to look as though they had spokes. By about 2000 B.C., war chariots, which had to be light and fast, had almost modern-looking spokes.

A wheel and axle—like the one you made—is a device for reducing friction. The forward motion of the travois continuously rolls the wheel onto new points of contact with the earth. Because the area of contact between the wheel and the earth at any point is small and brief, the friction is low.

The wheel was certainly one of humankind's greatest inventions, and it's hard to imagine life without wheels. Surprisingly, however, some ancient societies that invented the wheel never used wheels for transportation. In Central America, children were given toys with wheels, but there is no sign that anyone built a full-size cart or wagon. In some parts of the Middle East, after someone invented a pack saddle for camels, people stopped using wheeled vehicles and relied on camels. Ironically, in the area where the wheel was invented, the wheel was then abandoned as a way of moving people and things!

INVENTOR'S CHALLENGE

Did the wheels on your travois tend to slide off the dowels? Can you invent two ways to keep the wheels in place while still allowing them to turn freely?

Materials
rubber bands
modeling clay

In the earliest Mesopotamian wheels, a peg driven through the wooden axle just beyond the wheel prevented the wheel from falling off. Later, cart and wagon makers used copper bolts instead of wooden pegs.

3 Shadoof

The Problem

You are a farmer in ancient Egypt, about 3000 B.C. The Nile River floods each year, bringing crucial water and rich soil to your dry land. Each summer, as the floodwaters retreat, you work hard to capture as much of this water as you can for your crops. You have been using leather buckets to carry the water up to your fields from the bank of the river, from the shallow ponds that the river leaves behind, and from the irrigation ditches you have dug. It's slow, exhausting work, though, and you start thinking: How can you lift water more quickly and with less effort?

Observations

You are familiar with balances, which you and other farmers use to weigh your grain harvest. A **balance** is made of a beam that pivots in the middle, with pans hanging by cords from either end of the beam. You fill the pan on one side with grain. Then, in the other pan, you add stones of a known weight. As you add stones, the pan with the grain rises. This makes you think. . . .

MATERIALS

forked branch 2 to 3 feet (60 to 90 cm) long
Styrofoam or paper cup
pencil
string
scissors
water

straight branch (or dowel) about 2 feet (60 cm) long
variety of pebbles and stones
wide packing tape
bowl

Experiment

1. Push the unforked end of the forked branch firmly into the ground.

2. Using a pencil, make three small holes in the cup at about equal distances apart, near the rim. Cut three pieces of string, each about 6 inches (15 cm) long.

3. Thread one end of a piece of string through one of the holes in the cup, and tie it in a knot. Repeat this process with the other two strings. Fill the cup half full with water. Gather the other ends of the strings together, and experiment with lifting the cup of water from the ground by pulling straight up on

the strings. Move the cup from one spot to another. Note how much effort it takes.

4. Tie the ends of the strings around one end of the straight branch or dowel.

5. Rest the middle of the straight branch across the **V** in the upright branch.

6. Use your finger to push down on the other end of the stick and raise the cup. How much effort does it take? Experiment by moving the stick across the **V**. If you move the cup closer to the **V**, how much effort does it take to raise the cup? How about if you move the cup farther from the **V**?

7. Rest the middle of the straight branch across the **V** again. Gather as many stones as you think are equal to the weight of the cup and water. Use the packing tape to tape stones to the underside of the other end of the straight branch. Add or remove stones until they balance the cup. Is it easier now to lift and move the water with your invention?

8. Put the bowl to one side, where the cup can reach it if you swivel the dowel. Now, tip the water out of the cup into the bowl. You've just invented an Egyptian *shadoof* to help you bring water to your fields!

The straight branch or dowel is acting as a lever. A **lever** is any bar that tilts on a fulcrum. In this case, the **fulcrum** (the point on which a lever turns or is supported) is the forked branch. If you apply a force on one end of a lever, the lever can do some useful work at the other end.

A simple machine such as the lever makes work easier because it changes the amount of force you need to provide to perform work. In the first part of this experiment, you saw that as you increased the amount of stick (and its weight) on your side of the fulcrum, you needed less of your own muscle power to lift the water. When you added enough stones to your side of the fulcrum, the downward force they exerted raised the water with hardly any of your effort. The more weight you add to your end of the lever, the less force you have to apply to get work done at the other.

Answers from the Past

The land of Egypt is dry. Only the Nile River makes farming possible in Egypt. On either side of the Nile, there is a swath of green farmland. Beyond the green, for miles and miles, is the pale yellow of desert sands.

Once a year, in the spring, the Nile floods. In ancient Egypt, this flooding was a great event. When the Nile overflowed its banks, it brought essential fresh water and spread a fresh covering of new, fertile soil over the underlying sand. As spring wore on, the waters slowly retreated.

As early as 2500 B.C., the Egyptians had become expert at building *irrigation systems,* which were intricate networks of reservoirs, canals, and ditches that would capture the spring floodwaters. With irrigation systems in place, farmers were able to continue to water their crops through the hot, dry summer.

Building irrigation canals was only the first step, though. Egyptian farmers still had to transport the water from the ditches to the crops. For thousands of years, they carried the water in leather or wood buckets.

About 1500 B.C., some unknown (to us) Egyptian had a new idea, perhaps inspired by seeing a balance used to weigh grain. This ancient Egyptian balanced one piece of wood across another that had a V at the top (just as you did).

He or she attached a leather bag or a clay pot to one end. At the other end, this farmer attached—probably with rope made of reeds—a stone or stones of equal weight to the bucket and water. With this device, which became known as the **shadoof,** positioned by an irrigation ditch (or by a temporary pond or the river itself), a farmer could lift bucket after bucket and transport them to the field, with relatively little effort.

> The Egyptians invented the *balance,* a device for measuring the weight of things, about 3500 B.C. At first they used stones of certain weights to balance the weight of the object or objects being weighed. Around 2000 B.C., as metalworking developed, they began to use standardized metal weights.

Think of how heavy a gallon jug of water is. Imagine how hard it would have been to lift and carry hundreds of those a day—as Egyptian peasants did—from an irrigation ditch to a field. The shadoof must have seemed like a miracle. Farmers still use the shadoof to irrigate fields in parts of Egypt, India, and other countries.

INVENTOR'S CHALLENGE

Using a series of shadoofs and bowls, see how far away or how high you can transport water.

Materials

- more sticks
- dowels
- cups
- strings
- stones, as in the original experiment

4 Catapult

The Problem

It is 350 B.C. and you are a Greek engineer. Your king, Philip II of Macedon (Alexander the Great's father), has set out to conquer many of the neighboring Greek city-states. Philip has had many great victories but also some terrible defeats (particularly against Thessaly). The Macedonian army has giant **crossbows** mounted on platforms, which send arrows, stones, and other objects into opposing armies. These weapons aren't powerful enough

or accurate enough for the king, though. He wants you to design a new, more powerful weapon to use against the enemy forces.

Observations

For thousands of years, people around the world had been using strands of fiber, such as vines or cotton or hemp, to hold or tie things together. Over time, people had discovered that twisting the strands together made a rope that was stronger and easier to use than straight vines. They also discovered that if they twisted a strand of fiber, it had a tendency to untwist.

MATERIALS

two long skewers, each having a circular loop at one end

large, thick rubber band

spoon

marshmallow or small ball of paper

pencil

What these ancient people had discovered was that subjecting a fiber strand to **torsion**, which means twisting, gives the strand **potential energy**. When the ends of a twisted strand are released, that potential energy becomes actual (or **kinetic**) **energy**. The strand untwists until it returns to its original, straight state. If twisted tightly, a strand can untwist with great force.

Experiment

1. Push one of the skewers into the ground until only about 6 inches (15 cm) shows above ground.

2. Push the second skewer into the ground about 6 inches (15 cm) from the first skewer.

3. Put a rubber band around the skewers about 1 inch (2.5 cm) below the skewers' loops. (You may have to adjust the height of the rubber band later.)

4. Stick the stem of the spoon between the two sides of the rubber band, with the bowl facing away from you. Rotate the spoon toward you and down so that it twists the rubber band. Keep rotating the spoon to twist the rubber band tightly.

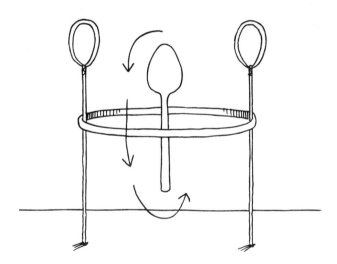

5. Hold the spoon parallel to the ground, with the bowl facing up. Put a marshmallow or a tightly wadded piece of paper in the bowl of the spoon.

6. Release the spoon. What happened? Can you think what else this machine needs?

7. Turn the skewers so that you can rest the pencil across them, through the loops.

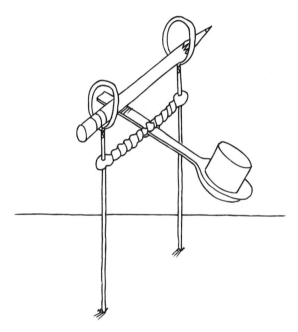

8. Stick the stem of the spoon between the two sides of the rubber band and wind it up, as you did in Step 4. Place the marshmallow or paper in the bowl of the spoon. Release the spoon. You've just created a Greek catapult!

Your catapult uses the power of torsion to send the marshmallow flying. By rotating the spoon, you twist the rubber band. When you release the spoon, all the potential energy in the twisted rubber band turns into kinetic energy.

Without the pencil, the spoon turned and turned until the rubber band untwisted. As you saw, the marshmallow was launched into the ground. With the pencil, the catapult worked. When the spoon hit the pencil, some of the energy was transferred to the marshmallow. The marshmallow flew straight through the air. It eventually fell to Earth because it encountered air resistance, which slowed it down, and gravity, which pulled it down. As long as the rubber band is still twisted tightly, there is still lots of potential energy in your catapult.

Answers from the Past

One of Philip's engineers invented a torsion device for launching stones and rocks in about 340 B.C. It used various fibers, including hair, sinews from animals, and plant materials, twisted into a rope to power a wooden pole that slammed into a heavy wood frame. At the end of the pole was a rock in a cuplike device or in a sling. The device was called a *katapultos,* which means "shield piercer" in Greek. The word **catapult** now is often used for any machine that launches missiles that fly through the air, whether they use torsion or other forces for their power.

Before the Greek catapult, all stone and arrow launchers used **tension** to power missiles at the enemy. In tension devices, such as a bow and arrow or a crossbow, potential energy is stored by pulling a straight piece of wood or other material into a bow shape. When the string or rope holding the wood in a bow shape is released, the wood straightens suddenly, the potential energy becomes kinetic energy, and an arrow or stone flies out from the bow. Before designing the catapult, the Greeks developed and used the *gastraphete,* which was a large, powerful crossbow mounted horizontally on a stand.

The torsion catapult was a significantly better missile launcher than the tension gastraphete. It was more powerful and more accurate. A 5-foot (1.5-meter) gastraphete could send a 3-ounce (85-gram) arrow about 150 yards (138 meters). A torsion catapult with a 7-foot (2.2-meter) arm could send a 10-pound (4.5-kg) rock more than twice as far.

About 200 B.C., the Romans borrowed the invention from the Greeks, and over the course of 600 years, they refined and improved it in many ways. They used lighter versions for

field warfare and heavier versions for attacking castles. A four-ton catapult could launch a 60-pound (27-kg) rock 500 yards (462 meters, the length of five football fields).

Ultimately, the Roman catapult changed the nature of warfare. Castles that had once been invulnerable could be seriously damaged by flying boulders. People were defenseless before such missiles. It became more difficult for castle defenders to outlast their attackers.

INVENTOR'S CHALLENGE

Catapults were very heavy. What if your enemy was far away or on the move? Build a catapult in a frame that can be easily moved around.

Materials

box of Tinker Toys, Legos, or other building kit

5 Counterweight Trebuchet

The Problem

You are an engineer in the army of Manuel I, the Emperor of Byzantium (which is roughly modern-day Turkey), in about A.D. 1150. Manuel is desperate to win back territory for his shrinking empire. His extensive domain has been reduced by attacks from all sides: the Normans in the west, the Serbs in the north, and the Turks in the east. Manuel has asked you to look at the army's siege machines to see what you can do to improve them.

Observations

The Byzantine army uses **traction trebuchets** *(treh-byuh-shets),* which are designed to shoot rocks over a distance and used most often to attack castles. These devices are, in essence, giant seesaws made from trees that were trimmed of their branches. Instead of two even sides, though, these seesaws have one long side and one short side. At the end of the long side, which rests on the ground, a rock is placed in a scoop or a sling. On the short end, which is up in the air, there are dozens—and sometimes hundreds—of ropes hanging down. When it is time to launch the rock, a soldier is assigned to each rope. Then, on command, the

soldiers yank the short end down. The long end rises suddenly, and the rock takes off through the air.

You notice, though, that it is hard to keep the traction trebuchet going in the heat of battle. Soldiers get tired. Some are killed. After a while, commanders don't know what targets the rocks will hit, if any, because they don't know how hard the soldiers will pull on the ropes on any particular shot. There must be a better way. . . .

All trebuchets use a *lever* (a bar) that rests unevenly on a *fulcrum* (the object on which the lever pivots) to throw a heavy load. It takes a lot of energy to overcome the inertia of the heavy rock. **Inertia** is the tendency of any object to remain at its current speed, which in the case of the rock is zero.

In a traction trebuchet, the energy is provided by the soldiers pulling down their end of the lever. (*Traction*, in this usage, means pulling.) The soldiers transfer their energy via the lever to the rock. The rock's inertia is overcome, and it flies toward the enemy. In a **counterweight trebuchet**, as you will see, gravity provides the energy to counteract the inertia of the heavy load.

MATERIALS

four metal skewers (either straight ones or ones with a loop at the top)

two ¼-inch (1-cm) diameter dowels 12 inches (30 cm) long

four small screw eyes

string

spoon

tape

marshmallow or marble

about a dozen washers

Experiment

1. Push two of the skewers into the ground at an angle, forming a triangle about 8 inches (20 cm) high at the highest point. Make the tops of the skewers overlap by an inch or so, or make their loops line up, as shown.

2. Repeat Step 1 with the other two skewers, to form another triangle parallel to the first and about 6 inches (15 cm) away from it.

3. Rest one of the dowels (which we'll call the crosspiece) across the tops of the triangles or through the loops.

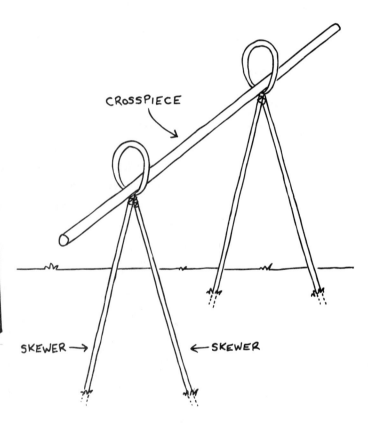

CROSSPIECE

SKEWER →   ← SKEWER

4. About 3 inches (8 cm) from one end of the other dowel (which we'll call the beam), twist in a small screw eye. The eye should be parallel to the beam. About 3¾ inches (10 cm) away from the same end, twist in another screw eye. The eye of this one, too, should be parallel to the dowel.

5. Twist a screw eye into the end of the beam closest to the other screw eyes. Attach three pieces of string to this screw eye. The pieces of string should be long enough to reach the ground when the beam is on the crosspiece.

6. Rest the beam across the crosspiece between the screw eyes. Tie a piece of string between the parallel screw eyes so that the beam cannot slip off the crosspiece.

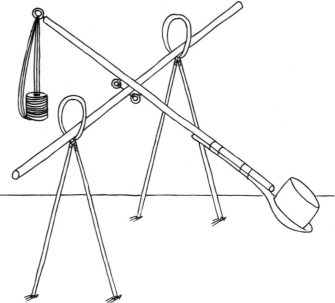

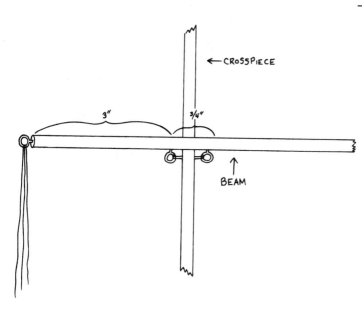

7. With tape, attach the spoon to the long end of the beam. Make sure the spoon faces up. Put a marshmallow or a marble on the spoon.

8. Hold the ends of all three strings, or hold one of the strings and have two friends hold the other strings. On the count of "three," pull the strings down. You've launched a *traction trebuchet!*

9. Now, make a stack of about 10 washers. Gather the three strings together and thread them through the stack. Secure the washers by tying the ends of the strings back to the screw eye. Leave several inches of string between the beam and the washers.

10. Reload your trebuchet, and hold the spoon to the ground. When you're ready, release the spoon. Now you've launched a counterweight trebuchet!

Answers from the Past

The Chinese invented the traction trebuchet between 400 and 200 B.C. With a team of men pulling at the ropes, they were able to launch 130-pound (59-kg) rocks up to 450 feet (137 meters). (That's the equivalent of launching an average high school boy over the length of one-and-a-half football fields.) Over the following centuries, this Chinese invention spread eastward through the Middle East and then to Europe.

The problem with traction trebuchets (as you may have discovered) is that it is hard to get people to pull all at the same time. It was hard to predict how far a rock would go because the pulling force would change as soldiers grew tired or were killed. Also, the soldiers launching rocks could have been put to better use shooting arrows or fighting in hand-to-hand combat.

The counterweight trebuchet solved these problems. It combined the force of gravity and heavy weights to provide the energy to launch the stones. Counterweight trebuchets used huge wooden buckets—some were as big as a cottage—holding rocks, sand, and debris to provide the weight at the short end. The counterweight trebuchet was a very effective siege machine. It could launch stones as large as 200 pounds (91 kg)—quite capable of doing serious damage to castle walls—over the length of three football fields (900 feet or 274 meters).

Sometimes, though, the attackers used trebuchets simply to demoralize a castle's defenders. They launched rotting, dead animals over the walls. If the attackers had captured any of the castle's inhabitants (a courier sent to get help, for example, or someone caught foraging for food), they might also launch that person, alive (for the moment), over the castle walls.

The earliest counterweight trebuchet mentioned in written records is one used by Manuel's army in 1165. No one knows exactly who invented it, but it served Manuel well. He was able to recapture territory that he had lost in the Balkans in Central Europe and at Antioch, capital of the ancient land of Syria, on the southern end of his empire. Nothing, though, could save the Byzantine Empire from the Crusaders, who sacked its capital, Constantinople (now Istanbul), in 1204.

INVENTOR'S CHALLENGE

Using the counterweight trebuchet, can you change the marshmallow's **trajectory** (path through the air) by increasing or reducing the number of washers you use? How far can you launch the marshmallow?

6 Archimedes Screw

The Problem

You are a Greek mathematician and inventor who lives in the town of Syracuse on the coast of Sicily, an island in the Mediterranean Sea, in the third century B.C. Many people in your town make their living from the sea, by either fishing or trading, in wooden ships.

The wooden planks of Syracusan watercraft are carefully joined and sealed, but inevitably some water leaks through the joints. In large ships, water gathers in the ship's **bilge,** an empty space far below the deck of the ship. To empty the water from a ship's bilge, sailors form a line from the bilge to the deck. The first sailor dips a bucket into the bilge and passes it up the line of sailors to the deck. The last sailor in line empties the bucket into the sea. Moving water in this way is a slow and labor-intensive process. You wonder: Is there an easier way to move water uphill?

Observations

You know that it is easier to push or roll a heavy object up a ramp than to try to lift it straight up. As a mathematician, you have studied ramps (which in geometry are called **inclined planes**). You have also studied and written about the geometry of circles, spheres, and spirals.

MATERIALS

empty, clear 1-liter plastic bottle

scissors

about 18 inches (45 cm) of ½-inch (1.25-cm) thick foam weather stripping with adhesive backing (available at a hardware store)

12-inch (30-cm) piece of approximately 1-inch (2.5-cm) diameter dowel

transparent tape

small, dried beans (navy beans, black-eyed peas, or pinto beans are good)

cereal bowl or other shallow container

water

food coloring

adult helper

Experiment

1. Ask your adult helper to cut off the top and bottom of the empty plastic bottle. Then ask your helper to cut the remaining plastic cylinder lengthwise. After the lengthwise cut is made, the plastic cylinder will curl around itself, forming a narrower cylinder about 6 inches (15 cm) long.

2. Peel the backing off of a few inches of one end of the weather stripping. Starting at one end of your dowel, wrap the stripping around the dowel in a spiral. The space between each rung of the spiral should be about ¾ inch (2 cm). Continue to peel the backing off the stripping as you spiral the stripping along the dowel. Continue the spiral until the length of dowel covered by stripping is equal to the length of the plastic cylinder.

3. Uncurl the cylinder enough to fit the dowel with its weather-stripping spiral into the cylinder. While you hold the dowel, have your adult helper adjust the plastic cylinder around it so that it fits snugly around the dowel, but not so snugly that you can't turn the dowel inside the cylinder. Tape the cut edge of the cylinder in place along the outside of the cylinder.

4. Take the dowel out of the cylinder. Use a long piece of tape to cover the cut edge on the inside of the cylinder so that the cylinder is smooth on the inside.

5. Pour enough dried beans into the small bowl so that the beans are about 2 inches (5 cm) deep.

6. Put the dowel into the cylinder. Put the end of the cylinder into the bowl, and hold the dowel at a small slope (no more than 30°). Turn the dowel in the direction that will lift the beans up the spiral. Keep turning until the beans come out the other end. You've made an Archimedes screw!

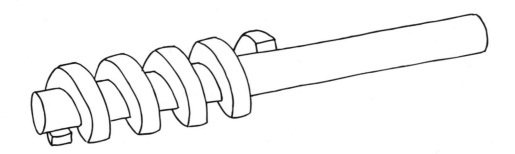

7. Empty the bowl, and put water into it. Add some food coloring. Try to lift water with the screw. (Your success will depend on how tightly the cylinder fits around the dowel.)

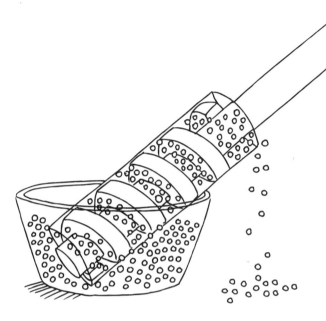

Answers from the Past

Archimedes was a great mathematician and inventor who lived in Greece in the third century B.C. We know about Archimedes's great mathematical discoveries because he wrote about them, but Archimedes didn't bother to write about his clever inventions, including the water screw and the block and tackle (see Chap-ter 7). However, we know from stories other people passed down that he invented these devices.

No one knows for certain what problem inspired Archimedes to invent the water screw. One story says that he invented it to empty water from the bilges of ships, just as in the problem posed at the beginning of this chapter. Another story is that Archimedes, on a visit to Egypt early in his career, was inspired by observing a rotating scoop device that Egyptian farmers used to transport water from the Nile River to their fields.

Archimedes had a mind well-prepared to solve the problem of moving water uphill. He had studied geometry and had begun the serious study of **mechanics,** which deals with the effect of forces on things. He understood that if a person applied force to an inclined plane, the inclined plane would perform action or *work*. Archimedes's understanding of inclined planes helped him to solve the problem of how to move water upward.

He reasoned that if you could wrap an inclined plane around a cylinder and apply some muscle power to turn the cylinder, water caught on the inclined plane would move upward. The ridge on any screw (the *thread*) is actually an inclined plane twisted into a three-dimensional spiral. In your experiment, when you apply force to one end of the screw (by turning it), the result is that beans or water move up a long inclined

An inclined plane can help you perform work. It can also make work easier. Imagine you're a hiker with a heavy backpack who wants to get to the top of a steep hill. The hill has a 50-foot (15-meter) vertical cliff on one side and a 500-foot (152-meter) gentle slope on the back side. If you climb the cliff, you only need to travel 50 feet, but you know it will be an exhausting climb. If you walk up the gentle back slope you will have to cover more distance, but you'll hardly be winded when you reach the top. The inclined plane reduces the effort to take each individual step—but you have to take a lot more steps.

plane. An inclined plane transforms the twisting force of your hand into the work of lifting the beans or water.

One of the simplest examples of an inclined plane performing work is the plow. When a farmer pushes or pulls a *wedge* (which is an inclined plane that moves) through the earth, the wedge pushes dirt aside so that seeds can be planted.

Archimedes's water screw is still used in Egypt and other parts of the less–developed world. His invention is still used in the developed world, too, in certain factory operations.

INVENTOR'S CHALLENGE

Another ancient water-lifting device was a vertical waterwheel that had buckets to catch and lift water. Use the following materials to make a waterwheel that lifts water.

Materials

round-barreled pencil

two 8-inch (20-cm) plastic disposable plates

tape

thin nail (to make holes in the paper plates)

light-gauge wire (thin enough to be cut with scissors)

scissors

paper cups for bathroom dispensers, cut down to a 1-inch (2.5-cm) height

CLUES

Use the pencil as an axle between the two plates. The cups need to swivel between the plates; otherwise all the water will spill out!

[7] Block and Tackle

The Problem

It is about 250 B.C., and you are that same famous Greek mathematician and inventor who invented the water screw, Archimedes (see Chapter 6). You have become good friends with King Hiero who rules the city of Syracuse on the island of modern-day Sicily. Hiero has heard you boast that with a few simple tools, you could move any object, no matter how heavy, and he has issued a friendly challenge to you to prove it.

Syracuse is a great port, and the city is full of ships, boats, sailors, and fishermen. One of the most difficult chores for any sea captain is pulling a ship ashore for repairs. The only way to do it is to attach ropes to the ship and command a team of people (often slaves) to haul it up onto the sand. If you could pull a ship up single-handedly, that feat would surely answer the king's challenge....

Observations

You have watched workers on the docks of Syracuse loading ships with goods for trade. They attach a heavy object to a rope that runs through a pulley fixed to the end of a beam that sticks out from the top of a building. By pulling down on the rope, they can lift the object up onto the ship's deck.

A single pulley attached to a structure is called a **fixed pulley**. It allows you to lift something up by pulling down. With a fixed pulley, you can add the weight of your body to your muscle power to raise a heavy load. A fixed pulley puts gravity on your side.

You have also experimented with levers. You were the first person to explain how levers decrease the effort needed to move a load. You realized that the longer the lever is on one side of the fulcrum, the easier it is to lift an object on the other side. "Give me but one firm spot on which to stand," you have claimed, "and I will move the Earth."

Now you see that a combination of pulleys and ropes can act like levers to reduce the effort needed to lift heavy loads.

MATERIALS

two chairs
broom or mop
thick, but bendable, wire (copper wire is good)
ruler
wire cutters
four empty spools of thread
several feet of strong string
beanbag or other small, heavy toy
scissors
toy bucket or small basket with a handle

Experiments

1. Lay the broom or mop across the backs of two chairs.

2. Measure and cut about 12 inches (30 cm) of wire, and slip one of the spools onto it. Then bend and twist the wire into a rectangular

shape with a hook at the top, as shown. Make sure the spool turns freely on the holder (called a *block*). Hang the block over the broom handle.

3. Tie a couple of feet (about 60 cm) of string to the handle of the basket. Put the basket on the floor, and put something in it (a small beanbag toy, for example). Pass the string over the spool, and pull down, as shown. You've made a fixed pulley!

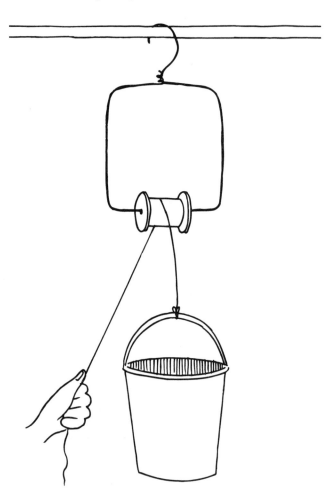

4. Now, make another block (see Step 2). Leave the first block on the broomstick. Hook the second block onto your basket, so that it is upside-down. Untie the piece of string from the basket, and tie it to the top of your first block. Then, thread the string (which is known as a *tackle*) around the spools, as shown. Pull the basket up. Is it easier to lift? You've made a **block and tackle**!

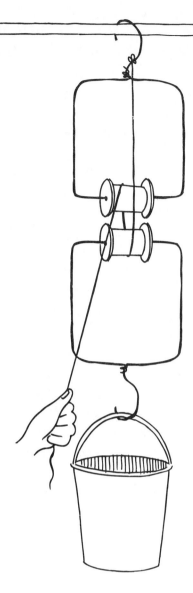

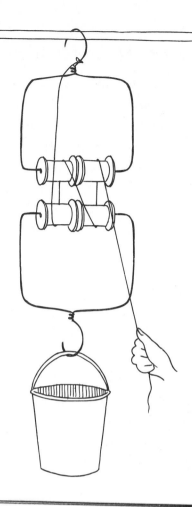

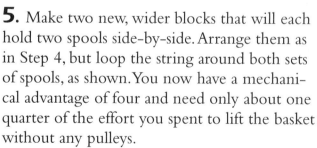

5. Make two new, wider blocks that will each hold two spools side-by-side. Arrange them as in Step 4, but loop the string around both sets of spools, as shown. You now have a mechanical advantage of four and need only about one quarter of the effort you spent to lift the basket without any pulleys.

A fixed pulley simply changes the direction of the effort you make to lift an object. A pulley that is attached to the object to be lifted (rather than to a structure) is called a **moveable pulley**. A moveable pulley can multiply the force you apply to lifting: It gives you a **mechanical advantage**. One moveable pulley gives you a mechanical advantage of two: With the same effort, you can lift a load that is twice as heavy.

The more moveable pulleys you add, the greater the mechanical advantage you gain ... until the additional friction created by the ropes in the pulleys offsets the mechanical advantage. A block and tackle of six pulleys, which would enable you to lift 600 pounds (272 kg) as easily as you could lift 100 pounds (45 kg) without it, is about the practical limit for pulleys.

Answers from the Past

It appears that Archimedes really did respond to a friendly challenge from King Hiero. (No one knows for sure because there are no eyewitness accounts, only stories written hundreds of years after Archimedes's death.) It is said that he single-handedly pulled a three-masted ship—with its crew and cargo!—up from the water by attaching a block and tackle to the boat and to a pier.

> **C**ould Archimedes really have pulled a three-masted ship out of the water by himself? Even a six-pulley block and tackle won't allow just one person to pull up such a heavy load. Either Archimedes had some help or, in the telling and retelling of the story over the centuries, a small fishing boat grew into a large ship!

During most of Archimedes's life, Syracuse was at peace with its neighbors. In 215 B.C., however, the Romans launched a naval attack against the city. Syracuse was protected by thick stone walls built right at the water's edge. As the Roman ships sailed toward the city, the Syracusan defenders used catapults (under the direction of Archimedes) to launch stones at the Roman ships. (See Chapter 4 for more on catapults.)

The Romans weathered this barrage, however, and sailed their ships to the base of the walls. Marcellus, the Roman commander, thought he had it made: The Syracusan catapults couldn't hit his ships at such close range. He called for the special scaling ladders covered with tough canopies (to protect his men from rocks dropped from the top of the walls), which he had ordered made. His men leaned the ladders against the walls, ready to climb them.

Marcellus hadn't counted on Archimedes's ingenuity, however. The next thing the Romans saw was a beam swinging out over the top of the fort's walls. At the end of the beam was a pulley. Dangling from the pulley was an enormous boulder. The Syracusans released the boulder (said to weigh about 600 pounds (272 kg), destroyed the ladders, and nearly sank the ship holding the ladders as well.

INVENTOR'S CHALLENGE

Elevators use pulleys to lift the weight of elevator cabs and the people in them. Can you make your block and tackle into an elevator that can lift the weight in your basket, so that you barely have to pull the other end of the string?

Materials
   materials from your original experiment
   a second basket in which you can put various objects to balance the weight of the beanbag, toy, or other object you put in the first basket

CLUES
An elevator cab has a heavy wire cable attached to its roof, which goes over a pulley underneath the roof of the building. To balance the weight of the elevator cab and the people inside, a huge counterweight is attached at the other end of the wire cable. A motor drives the cable through the pulley to move the elevator cab, but the motor only has to use enough power to lift the difference between the cab and the counterweight.

[8] Mechanical Fan

The Problem

You are a wheat farmer in northern China in the second century B.C. It is harvest time, and you have cut down the tall stalks of wheat with their heavy heads of grain. Now your task is to **winnow** your harvest. That is, you must separate the **chaff** (the stalks and the husks) from the valuable wheat seeds. In your village, people use the wind to winnow the harvest. When the wind is strong, they place the harvest in wide, shallow winnowing baskets. Then they toss the wheat into the air. The wind blows the light chaff away, and the heavy seeds fall back down into the basket.

One problem with this age-old method is that it's slow. Worse, you are at the mercy of the weather: You have to wait for a strong wind before you can finish winnowing your harvest. Wouldn't it be great if you could create your own steady wind? You could winnow your wheat any time. . . .

Observations

You know how to make a fan out of rice paper, which you wave to create a breeze that helps you keep cool.

You have a wheelbarrow on your farm, so you are familiar with the wheel as it turns on an axle.

You're a clever girl. You turn your wheelbarrow over and attach paper fans, at an angle, to the wheel. With the palm of your hand, you turn the wheel. As you imagined, the turning wheel creates a flow of air. The breeze you've created, though, is weak because you can't turn the wheel fast enough. It's tiring, too, to keep the wheel turning, and hard to maintain a steady rate. How can you get the wheel to turn faster and more steadily, with less effort?

Materials

drawing compass

cardboard

scissors

ruler

posterboard

tape

glue

pencil

an 8-inch (21-cm) piece of ½-inch (1.25-cm) wooden dowel

Styrofoam cup at least 5 inches (12 cm) tall

rice or stones to weight the cup

8-inch (21-cm) piece of wire (You need to be able to put two sharp bends in the wire, but it should otherwise be as rigid as possible.)

index card

Experiments

1. Use the drawing compass to draw two circles, each 3½ inches (9 cm) in diameter on the cardboard. Cut out the two cardboard circles.

2. Cut a strip of posterboard about 10 inches (25 cm) long and 1 inch (2.5 cm) wide. Bend it into a loop, and tape it closed.

3. Tape a cardboard circle to each side of the posterboard loop, as shown. This is your fan base.

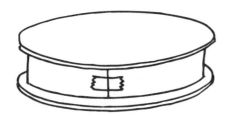

4. Use the drawing compass to draw a 16-inch (40-cm) diameter circle on the posterboard. Cut out the circle. Trim the circle to form five blades, as shown. Give each blade a slight bend at an angle, as shown. Glue the center of the fan to the fan base.

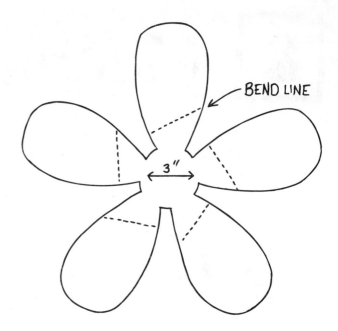

5. With a sharp pencil, make holes in the center of both sides of the fan base. Enlarge the holes with your finger. Push your dowel into the hole. It should fit snugly. Tape the dowel to the fan base so that about 1 inch (2.5 cm) sticks out one side, as shown.

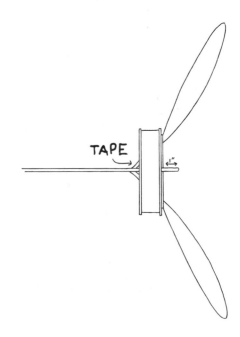

6. Using the pencil, poke two holes in the cup, a little below the rim. The holes should be directly opposite each other. Enlarge the holes with your finger. Push the long end of the dowel through the holes. Make sure the holes in the cup are big enough so the dowel turns freely. Pour stones or rice into the bottom of the cup to prevent it from tipping.

7. Place the cup on the edge of the table so the fan can turn. Spin the fan with your finger. Feel a breeze? (Figure out which way to turn the fan so the breeze blows away from the cup.) What problems do you discover while turning the fan this way?

8. Bend the wire in two places, as shown. The middle piece (the *crank*) should be about 2 inches (5 cm) long. The other pieces should be about 3 inches (8 cm) long.

9. Tape the wire onto the dowel, as shown.

10. Bend the index card lengthwise to form a ½-inch (1.25-cm) diameter tube. Tape the tube closed, and slip it onto the handle. (The tube makes it easier to hold and turn the handle.)

11. Hold the handle, and turn the crank. (It may help to hold the cup in place with your other hand.) You've made an ancient Chinese mechanical fan! Feel the breeze, and see how steady you can make it.

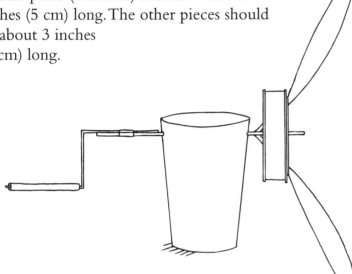

Answers from the Past

All over the world, for the thousands of years since people began harvesting grains, they have separated wheat from chaff (or rice from hulls) by tossing their harvest into the air and letting the wind winnow it. Many cultures have invented special baskets shaped for this activity.

In the second century B.C., the Chinese invented the crank and handle.

The mechanical fan you just made is based on a type of simple machine called a **wheel and axle.** Wheel-and-axle machines operate on the same principle as the lever. (See Chapters 3 and 5.) In this case, the dowel is the fulcrum, the fan blades are one side of the lever, and the crank is the other side of the lever.

Turn the crank handle one full turn. Compare the distance your hand traveled to the distance the ends of the fan blades traveled. In the same amount of time, the blades traveled a lot farther. Therefore, they must have traveled faster (while creating the nice breeze)!

The wheel-and-axle arrangement magnifies your hand's speed into the faster speed of the fan. In physics, however, you don't get something for nothing. You have to apply more force to the crank to get the increased speed of the fan in return. Fortunately, the fan is so light, and a crank is such a comfortable device for the human hand to use, you hardly feel the extra effort. In addition, with a crank and handle, you can apply your effort steadily, which makes the fan turn steadily.

They first used it in the winnowing fan, which proved to be a great labor- and time-saving device. Europeans developed their first crank and handle about 1,100 years later, in the ninth century A.D., to turn a grindstone to sharpen swords. The Europeans continued to winnow their wheat with baskets until about 1700, when Dutch sailors brought the Chinese winnowing fan back to Holland.

INVENTOR'S CHALLENGE

We use the crank and handle to perform all kinds of work. A crank and handle opens a casement window, turns the wheels on your bicycle, and winds up the fishing line on a fishing rod's reel. Some old-fashioned pencil sharpeners also use a crank and handle. Take off or cut off the fan blades of the mechanical fan you just made. Use your imagination and make a new device that accomplishes some task when you turn the handle.

PART II

Inventions Involving Chemical Changes

Chemical changes—the transformation of one substance into another through molecular change—constantly occur around us and within us. Plants use a chemical reaction called **photosynthesis** to turn sunlight, water, and carbon dioxide into the **carbohydrates** they need to survive and grow. Our stomachs contain chemical acids that break down the food we eat into the proteins, fats, and carbohydrates that our cells need to function.

People have used chemical reactions for their benefit for thousands of years. Ancient people made ceramics, which involved changing the chemical structure of clay by heating, and they preserved food by smoking or salting it. They decorated the walls of their caves, their bodies, and their clothes with paints and dyes created by chemical reactions. Later, they learned to manufacture glass and paper, to prepare long-lasting inks, and to combine copper and tin to make bronze.

Today, many industries make products that rely on chemical changes. The detergents you use to wash dishes are made by mixing benzene and hydrocarbons. Rubber for tires is a mixture of heated latex and sulfur. Plastics are the result of interactions among many different chemicals. Chemists can make plastic products as different as car bumpers and sandwich wrap by varying the mixture of chemical ingredients.

Most modern medicines are *synthetic,* meaning made by human beings. Chemists create them by combining the molecules of different chemicals in new ways. Almost all modern dyes and many perfumes are created in chemical laboratories.

9 | Tempera Paint

The Problem

Imagine you are an artist in prehistoric times. You draw your pictures of woolly mammoths, horses, bears, and other animals on the walls of underground caves where your tribe meets before its hunting expeditions. To make your drawings, you use white chalk scraped from cliffs, red and yellow clay scooped from the ground, and blackened, burned wood (charcoal) left in the campfire.

Your colors are vivid, but they are powdery, and your drawings rub off easily. So, you wonder: What can I add to my colored powders to make them last?

Observations

You have already discovered that mixing chalk, clays, and charcoal with water or your own spit makes these materials easier to spread on a wall. These materials are **pigments,** which means coloring materials that don't dissolve in water. So, when the water or your spit dries, your artistic work is as fragile as a chalk drawing.

You have noticed that *sap,* a clear liquid that oozes from certain trees, is clear and dries hard. You have also noticed that when bird and duck eggs smash on the ground, the egg mixture also dries to a shiny, hard finish. What would happen if you mixed your pigments with sap or egg goo?

MATERIALS

several sticks of chalk (thick sidewalk chalk is best, colored if you like)

two or more sheets of dark construction paper

cheese grater

plate

egg

cup

small paintbrush

Experiments

1. Take a piece of chalk, and do a quick drawing on a piece of paper. Then brush your hand across your drawing, and see how easy it is to smear your work.

2. Hold a cheese grater over a plate, and rub a stick of chalk against the smallest holes in the grater. Be careful to keep your fingers away from the sharp cutting edges of the grater.

3. After you have accumulated a small pile of chalk dust, add several drops of water, and stir to make a thick paste. Add more chalk dust if the paste is too thin. Add more water if the paste is too thick.

4. Crack an egg into a cup, and then pour off the egg white. Mix the yolk thoroughly. (Don't worry if some egg white gets mixed in with the yolk.) Paint a little egg yolk on a piece of paper so you can see how clear and shiny it is when it dries. (Note: Always wash your hands after handling raw eggs. They may contain harmful bacteria.)

5. Add a few drops of the egg-yolk mixture to the chalk paste, until you have a brushable liquid. This is **egg tempera** paint, one of the oldest paints known to humankind!

6. Dip your brush in the paint, and paint on a new piece of paper. When your painting dries, rub your hand across it. Does it smear?

Pigments are tiny bits of a colored material. Pigments don't dissolve in liquids the way salt dissolves in water. Instead they are suspended, unchanged, in the liquid. If the liquid is sap or egg yolk, when the liquid dries, it hardens around the pigment, trapping the tiny bits in their suspended state. Because the liquid binds the bits of pigment together, it is called a **binder**.

Answers from the Past

The earliest egg-tempera paintings were made on the walls of caves in southern France and northern Spain by humans who lived more than 20,000 years ago. These early artists also added tree sap and animal grease to their pigments, as binders to make paints. All of these paints were easy to spread and were less fragile than pigments applied directly to the wall.

Sometimes prehistoric artists applied a pigment and water or saliva mixture (called a **wash**) to the wall, using a brush or a finger. Sometimes they placed one of their hands flat against the wall and then blew the wash onto the wall, either directly from their mouths or possibly through a hollow plant stalk. These hand silhouettes appear frequently in certain ancient caves.

By 3000 B.C., humans had come up with new binders. People in the Middle East had discovered a natural glue, called **casein,** in milk, which made a good binder for paint. They also learned how to apply pigments to wet plaster walls, so that the pigments bound with the plaster and became a part of the wall's surface. Later, the ancient Greeks mixed pigments in heated wax and painted with it.

It wasn't for many thousands of years (probably around A.D. 500), however, that artists invented oil-based paints. Oil-based paints use oil as a binder. The clarity of the oil allows light to penetrate the paint and reflect from the surface beneath back through the paint to your eye. (Light reflects directly off the surface of tempera paints.) That is why oil-based paints look richer than watercolor or tempera paints.

Today, artists still use many of the prehistoric pigments and binders. Most house paints, though, are made from synthetic pigments and synthetic binders such as acrylic and vinyl. These binders are made of plastic, which means they are made of long chains of carbon-based molecules. These long chains of molecules can be made very tough, as well as flexible. Outdoor paints must be able to expand and contract with the heat and cold and to resist water. Paints with plastic binders hold up well under these conditions.

INVENTOR'S CHALLENGE

Try mixing some chalk and clay with different binders. Which paints dry into the brightest colors? Which are easiest to paint with? Experiment with new pigments to make different colored paints. Give your favorite a name, and send a sample to a crayon company!

Materials
chalks
clays
various binders (try gum arabic from a hobby shop)

Chalk is made of zillions of tiny, crushed, fossilized marine creatures. Linseed oil, one of the best oils for paint, is made of the seeds of the flax plant. (The fibers of the flax plant are used to make a fabric called linen.) Gum arabic comes from the sap of the acacia tree, which grows in Africa, Australia, and Asia.

Over time, people discovered lots of new pigments. They continued to use the clays that the most ancient artists used, but they also discovered that they could get different colors from them by roasting the clays. Burnt umber, a familiar color in a crayon box, is just that: a clay called umber, which is burned to make it reddish-brown!

Blues and greens were harder to come by. Green was first made from a ground-up mineral called malachite, which is a compound of copper. Lapis lazuli is a semiprecious blue gem found in Iran, Afghanistan, and China. Artists found they could grind it up to use as a beautiful pigment, but it was very expensive. Much later, in the 1500s, artists charged extra for a painting with blue in it.

10 Vegetable Dye

The Problem

It is about 3000 B.C., and you are a weaver in the city of Harappa in the Indus Valley, in what is today India and Pakistan. You take fibers from the outer ball of fluff surrounding the cotton seed, separate the fibers, and spin them into thread. Cotton is naturally off-white, so you often **dye** (permanently color) the thread before weaving it into fabric.

Dyes and dyed cloth are very valuable items to trade, especially when foreigners arrive in the city. Dyers like you are always looking for new dyes to make cloth in colors never seen before. Most dyers do their best to keep their recipes a secret, so that only they can produce a particular color.

You are constantly experimenting with the plants around you to see what colors you can produce. You use parts of the flowers of the safflower plant to make an orange dye and the roots of the madder plant to make a red. You would love to have a bright yellow color but haven't discovered how to make it. Where can you get such a color?

Observations

Others in your village experiment with the flowers, berries, and roots of plants, too. Some are looking for plants that add flavor to food. Others test plants to see whether they cure illnesses. Everyone knows that the plant kingdom is rich with possibilities. One of your neighbors has discovered that if she grinds up the root of the curcuma plant, it adds a wonderful spice to food. The root is a yellow color—would it make a dye?

MATERIALS

white wool yarn
scissors
water
1-cup (250-ml) liquid measuring cup
one or more small saucepans
adult helper
plastic apron to protect your clothes
measuring spoons
turmeric (available in the spice section of a
 grocery store)
stirring spoon
fork

Experiments

1. Cut three pieces of the yarn. Each piece should be about 6 inches (15 cm) long.

2. Put 1 cup (250 ml) of water in a saucepan.

3. Ask an adult to help you bring the water to a simmer. While you are waiting, put on your apron.

4. Add 1 teaspoon (5 ml) of turmeric and two pieces of yarn to the water. Stir.

5. After 2 minutes, ask your helper to use a fork to take out one piece of yarn. Rinse the yarn in tap water.

6. After 10 minutes, ask your helper to take out the other piece. Rinse it.

7. Add ¼ teaspoon (1 ml) of cream of tartar to the saucepan, and stir. Then add another piece of yarn. After 10 minutes, ask your helper to take out the yarn. Rinse it.

8. You've dyed yarn in much the way dyers did thousands of years ago! Did you notice any difference in the results of the different methods?

Answers from the Past

More than 5,000 years ago, people invented the first **textiles** (fabrics made out of woven *fibers*, strands of plant materials or animal hair). Many of the earliest pieces of fabric were dyed. At first, people must have tried to color the fabric with the clays and chalks that they used to decorate the walls of their houses and their bodies. Most of these substances, though, would have washed out of the fabrics.

t is rare to find fabrics from long ago because all fabrics and dyes decay over time, but one place they can be found is in mummy wrappings. The chemicals that the ancient Egyptians used to preserve a body also preserved fabric. Archaeologists have found linen made 5,000 years ago that was used to wrap mummies. The linen is still colored with safflower, madder, and other plant dyes.

Very soon after inventing textiles, people would have noticed that certain plant substances—such as berries, wet bark, pollen from flowers, and grass—made permanent marks on the fabrics. All over the world, starting about 3000 B.C., people experimented with the fruit, stems, flowers, and roots of plants to make dyes. This experimentation was a part of other experimenting with plants to make new foods, spices, or medicines.

As they experimented, people learned that certain plants were **direct dyes,** which meant they stained by themselves. Turmeric (the root of a curcuma plant, which is also used to spice food) is a direct dye first used in India about 3000 B.C. It produces a range of yellows, depending on the materials dyed.

Later, people discovered that some dyes—called **indirect dyes**—worked only when used in combination with certain other substances. Those other substances are known as **mordants.** People discovered that the bark of oak trees was a good mordant, as were tea, water made acid by rotting leaves, and vinegar. Alum, which is found in certain plant roots and as a mineral in the ground, has been a popular and effective mordant.

Indigo is another important vegetable dye. Indigo doesn't require a mordant, but dyers had to *decompose* (rot) it in water, dry it, and then dissolve it in an alkaline liquid (stale urine was often used!) before using it to dye cloth deep blue. Indigo was used to color blue jeans until a synthetic indigo became a cheaper alternative. The leaves of the indigofera plant have been used to produce blue since 2500 B.C. Madder, the root of a madder plant, is another indirect dye that was popular throughout the Middle East and Europe for thousands of years. The British Army soldiers couldn't have been called "Redcoats" by the American rebels if madder hadn't been around.

People extracted dyes from animals, as well as plants. About 1500 B.C., the Phoenicians, who lived on the Mediterranean Sea in what is today southern Lebanon, made a purple dye from the mucus of a particular shellfish. In Mexico, people found that a kind of louse (called a cochineal) that feeds on cactus made an excellent red dye when dried and crushed. It takes thousands of shellfish and cochineals, though, to dye one robe. As a result, the dyes were very expensive. Because only royalty could afford robes made with such dyes, purple and red became the colors of royalty.

The word *mordant* comes from the Latin word *mordere*, meaning to bite. A mordant helps a dye "bite" into fabric. Unlike direct dyes, which have a chemical structure that allows them to bind directly with the fibers in a fabric, indirect dyes do not chemically attach themselves to fibers. A mordant forms a chemical bond between the indirect dye and the fiber, linking the two together permanently.

INVENTOR'S CHALLENGE

Make a vegetable dye in your own custom color.

Materials

  saucepan
  apron
  white silk embroidery thread
  white wool yarn
  scissors
  spoon
  fork
  various dyestuffs such as red cabbage
    leaves, marjoram, onions, black tea,
    herbal tea, coffee, the *stamens* (the
    tall, threadlike parts inside the flower)
    of crocuses and dark tulips
  various additives: alum (available in the
    spice section of a grocery store), an iron
    pill or a daily vitamin with iron crushed
    and mixed with water, cream of tartar
    adult helper

CLUES

Experiment with some or all of the substances listed here. You will need an adult to help you simmer the dyestuffs in water. Vary the amount of time the silk thread or wool yarn simmers. Experiment with putting wool and silk in the same **dyebath** (the hot water mixed with a dyestuff): The same dyes produce different colors on different materials.

A number of companies sell some of the old natural dyes, such as madder, Osage orange, cutch (catechu), logwood, cochineal, and alkanet. Search the Internet using "natural dyes catalog" as a search term.

⑪ Iron-Gall Ink

The Problem

You are a monk in a monastery in Gaul (part of what is now France) some time in the twelfth century. At this time, all books are copied by hand, and your job as a **scribe** is to make copies of the classics of Greek and Roman literature. The "paper" you use is **parchment,** which is specially prepared animal skin.

The ink you are using—a deep black ink made of soot (from burned oil), water, and a little honey or glue—is a kind that has been used for thousands of years. It is difficult to work with, however, especially with your goose-quill pen. The honey or glue thins and thickens as the temperature of your room rises and falls, so the consistency of your ink changes. When the ink is too thick, it clogs your pen.

The other problem is that though the ink doesn't fade, it smudges easily. Even worse, it can easily be scraped off the parchment. In fact, the parchment you are using has faint remains of someone else's writing, which you have scraped off!

You wonder whether you could make an ink that is less expensive (the oil burned to make the fine soot costs a lot), easier to use, and more permanent.

Observations

At the monastery, some clothes are washed by boiling them in a large iron pot. From time to time, the white clothes come back a brownish color, and you know they were left to soak too long in the iron pot. You also know that dyers of textiles use water that has had oak galls soaking in it to make their dyes permanent. These two facts make you think. . . .

Oak galls are the bumps you find on many oak trees. The **galls** are created by certain flies or wasps. The female insect makes a hole in the oak tree's bark and lays her eggs. The hatched larvae feed on the tree and secrete a chemical irritant that causes the tree to create a growth. The growth protects the tree from the insects and the insects from hungry birds and other predators. When the larvae mature into adult insects, the insects chew their way out of the gall.

2. Put ½ cup (125 ml) of hot water from the tap into a mug. Put a tea bag in the water. Let the tea steep for at least 15 minutes.

3. Add the tea to the vinegar in the glass. Watch the color change: You've made an iron-gall ink, much like the ones invented in the Middle Ages!

4. Experiment with using a Q-tip or both ends of the paintbrush to write with your ink. To make a thicker ink, beat an egg yolk well, add a few drops to your ink, and stir. (Caution: Always wash your hands after handling raw eggs. They may contain harmful bacteria.)

MATERIALS

plastic apron or smock

1-cup (250-ml) liquid measuring cup

vinegar

small, stainless-steel bowl or pot

steel-wool pad that doesn't contain soap

glass (drinking)

hot tap water

mug

tea bag (filled with black, not herbal, tea)

Q-tips or a small paintbrush

paper

egg

Caution: This ink is permanent, so make sure you wear a smock, an apron, or old clothes.

Experiment

1. Pour 1 cup (250 ml) of vinegar into a bowl, and add the steel-wool pad. Make sure the vinegar covers the steel wool. Let it sit overnight. The next day, take out the steel wool, and throw it away. Pour ½ cup (125 ml) of this vinegar into a glass.

5. Your writing will look light at first. This kind of ink starts out pale, but it darkens over time.

Is this really ink and not just a temporary stain? After your writing dries, rub some water on it. What happens?

Answers from the Past

The ancient Egyptians were the first to develop ink for writing. That they were first is not surprising because they were also the first to invent a kind of paper—**papyrus** from the papyrus plant—about 3000 B.C. (See Chapter 12 for more about paper.) At the same time, they came up with a jet-black ink. They used soot as a pigment, which they mixed with water. To make the ink stick to the papyrus, they used a binder of glue, tree sap, or honey.

Carbon inks (those with pigments made of soot or charcoal) never faded, and they were easy to spread with the small brushes or frayed reeds that people in the ancient world used as pens. Carbon inks were common throughout the Middle East and Europe until the Middle Ages (and in Asia even longer). When people needed colors other than black, they turned to dyes, which they knew colored fabric. For brown, they used a dye from cuttlefish. For red, they used the roots of the madder plant, and for blue, they used the leaves of the indigofera plant. Many of these dye-based inks have faded over time, but the carbon inks are still as black as the day they were made.

> **T**he Chinese also developed a soot ink about the same time. The best soot, called *lamp-black*, was made from incompletely burning oil in a lamp.

We know that by A.D. 50, the Romans had discovered that a sheet of papyrus soaked in a solution of water and crushed oak galls would turn black wherever a solution with copperas (iron sulfate) dripped on it. A few Roman documents survive that may have been written with this iron-gall ink, but the ink didn't catch on. Then, knowledge of iron-gall ink was lost after the fall of the Roman Empire, about the year 500.

In the twelfth century, someone reinvented iron-gall ink. (The inventor was probably a monk. Monks were among the few people who knew how to read and write in the Middle Ages.) This time, iron-gall ink caught on. It helped that people learned to add a bit of dye to the ink to make their writing visible before the ink darkened. In addition, because iron-gall ink was more liquid than soot-based ink, it dried quickly and smudged less. It didn't clog quill pens. The ingredients were cheap and available everywhere. Best of all, because iron-gall ink penetrated the paper (which was replacing parchment at this time), it was truly permanent and couldn't be scraped off.

By the thirteenth century, iron-gall ink was Europe's primary ink. Iron-gall ink was used well into the twentieth century, when inks made with synthetic dyes became more popular.

> **H**ow did iron-gall ink work? Oak galls contain gallic and tannic acids. The copperas the Romans used contained iron. When the gallic and tannic acids mixed with the iron, they formed a chemical compound called ferrogallotannate. (In Latin, *ferr* means iron.) The ink darkened when the ferrogallotannate combined with oxygen in the air.
>
> Your ink works in almost the same way. The iron in the steel wool reacts with the tannic acid in the tea to form a compound called ferrotannate. (The vinegar you used prevents atoms of iron from combining with atoms of oxygen to form iron oxide—rust—instead of ferrotannate.) Your ink darkened when the ferrotannate combined with oxygen in the air. Your ink won't be as black as ink made with galls because gallic acid is better for producing color than is tannic acid.

Inventor's Challenge

Make your own inks from some or all of the following materials. You can mix materials for new colors. To see how permanent the various inks are, rub them with water after they've dried.

Materials

    water
    turmeric (a spice)
    coffee
    soot or charcoal
    red cabbage leaves
    maraschino cherry juice
    Kool-Aid
    pecan or walnut shells
    blueberry or grape jam
    adult helper
    raw egg or glue

Clues

Some materials need to be simmered in water, so ask an adult to help. You can use a little egg yolk or glue to thicken your ink.

12 Writing Paper

The Problem

It is about A.D. 100 at the Imperial Court in the ancient city of Beijing, China. You are Ts'ai Lun, the Inspector of Works, and must report to the emperor on ideas for improving manufacturing in China. You have already advised the emperor on ways to improve the production of swords and other armaments, and now you have turned your attention to materials for writing on.

Most Chinese *scribes* (people trained to write for the emperor and his court, as well as for citizens who cannot write) write on strips of silk, hemp, and other woven cloth. Woven cloth writing materials are expensive. You suspect there are ways to make cheaper, and perhaps better, writing materials.

Observations

At the workshops where the writing cloth is made, you notice that when the artisans cut their cloth into sheets, narrow strips are left over. When they trim the sheets to make them a uniform size, even smaller snippets, sometimes just threads, also fall to the floor. A servant comes and sweeps away all these small pieces of cloth.

You also visit the workshops of artisans who make a material used for everyday clothing and wrapping. The artisans pound mulberry tree bark and hemp stalks in water until the ingredients have become a thick mixture of water and tiny fibers. The artisans then pour the mixture onto mats, press the water out, and let the material dry. Finally, they cut the dried material into the desired size and shape.

MATERIALS

lint collected from a couple of dryer loads of light-colored, cotton clothes and sheets

blender

1-cup (250-ml) liquid measuring cup

water

adult helper

approximately 5- × 5-inch (12- × 12-cm) piece of fine-mesh nylon netting or wire screen

small baking dish

spoon or spatula

rolling pin (or large empty soda bottle)

sections of newspaper

optional: microwave oven or an iron

Experiment

1. Take the lint, and cut it up into small pieces. Put it in the blender. (The lint is your equivalent of the tiny pieces of fabric left on the floor by the workers who made writing cloth. Lint is made of tiny cotton fabric fibers beaten free from clothes as they tumble in the dryer.)

2. Add 1 cup (250 ml) of water to the lint. Have an adult help you blend the mixture for about 20 seconds—enough to make a relatively smooth **slurry** (a mixture of water and a substance that doesn't dissolve) of fibers.

3. Put the screen on the bottom of a baking dish. Carefully pour the slurry over the screen.

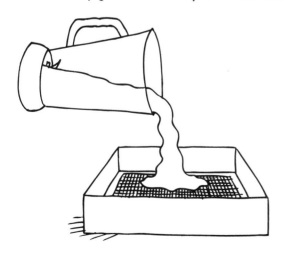

4. Use the spoon or spatula to spread the slurry evenly over the screen.

5. Lay a few sheets of newspaper on the table. Holding the edges of the screen, lift it directly up.

6. Lay the screen, slurry side up, on a section of newspaper. Cover it with another section of newspaper. With a rolling pin, roll flat these layers of newspaper and lint slurry.

7. Flip your screen-and-newspaper sandwich. Peel off the top layer of newspaper, and then peel off the screen. Your piece of paper will be stuck to the bottom layer of newspaper. You have made paper from tiny cloth fibers, in much the same way the ancient Chinese did!

8. Peel your paper from the newspaper. You can let the paper dry on a rack. If you want the paper to dry faster, you can put it in a microwave oven and heat it for about 1 minute at 50 percent power, or you can iron it (no steam) between two sections of dry newspaper. (Get adult help if you use the microwave or an iron.)

Answers from the Past

People have used many different materials to write on. As far as we know, the Mesopotamians were the first people to invent a written language, and they used sharpened sticks to make impressions in clay that they then baked. Other peoples have written on stones, leaves, and bark.

The earliest synthetic writing material that was lightweight but durable was a material made by the ancient Egyptians. About 3000 B.C., the Egyptians made a writing material called *papyrus* by laying long strips cut from the stem of the papyrus plant side by side and then placing other strips crosswise on top of them. Next, they wet the two layers of papyrus strips and pressed them together. When the papyrus dried, the sap from the papyrus held the strips together into a sheet. Papyrus was used not only in ancient Egypt, but also in ancient China, Greece, and Rome.

> **M**any of the ancient Greek and Roman texts were written on papyrus, and papyrus remained in use until the tenth century. The English word *paper* comes from *papyrus*. The word *Bible* comes from *bubloi*, the Greek word for the inner fiber of the papyrus plant.

Tanned animal hides have also been used as a material to write on for thousands of years. About 200 B.C., leather tanners in Pergamum (in modern Turkey) began to produce *parchment*, which was leather that was specially treated to be thin, flat, and smooth. The resulting off-white sheets became the writing material of choice in Europe from about the seventh through the eleventh centuries A.D.

None of these ancient writing materials was what we now call paper. *Paper* is defined as disintegrated plant fibers pressed and dried into a thin material. The ancient Chinese invented the first true paper, made of pounded, disintegrated fibers from the hemp plant and mulberry tree, about 100 B.C. Interestingly, the Chinese didn't use this paper to write on at first. Instead, they made it into clothes, and they wrapped packages in it. Huge quantities of pounded mulberry tree

> **I**n a text written in 93 B.C., an imperial guard recommended that a prince cover his nose with a piece of paper. So, another early use of paper was as a Kleenex!

bark were used to make all sorts of clothing, curtains, blankets, and other items.

In about A.D. 100, the emperor of China assigned a man named Ts'ai Lun to be the Inspector of Works. Ts'ai Lun's first assignment was to suggest improvements to the sword-making and armaments industry. Next, the emperor asked him to improve the manufacture of writing materials.

According to a Chinese historian writing 300 years after Ts'ai Lun's death, Ts'ai Lun "conceived the idea of making paper from the bark of trees, hemp waste, old rags, and fish nets" in A.D. 105. We know that material for clothing made from mulberry bark and hemp had already been invented, so perhaps Ts'ai Lun suggested that it could be used as a writing material. We do know that Ts'ai Lun conducted papermaking experiments because he gave the *mortar* (a device used for grinding) he had used to the emperor, who displayed it in the Imperial Museum. The oldest piece of paper with writing on it dates from A.D. 110.

Chinese techniques for making paper from rags spread westward, first to the Middle East, and then to Europe around 1100. Most paper today is made of wood pulp. Recycled paper is made by breaking down scraps of used paper and re-forming it into new sheets of paper. Some fancy writing papers still have cloth in them. These papers have a certain "rag" content.

INVENTOR'S CHALLENGE

Experiment with adding some of the following materials to your paper to give it scent, color, and a different texture.

Materials
herbs
shredded flower petals
food coloring

PART III

Inventions for Predicting the Weather

Let's say you lived in the sixteenth century, and you wanted to know how cold it was outside. You could check the horses' trough to see whether the water there had turned to ice. If you wanted to see how windy it was, you could toss some straw into the air to see how far the wind blew it. If you wanted to know what the weather would be tomorrow, you could ask your grandfather. When his bones ached, he claimed that meant rain was on the way.

In the seventeenth century, scientists first began to study the atmosphere methodically. They invented new instruments such as the *barometer* to measure air pressure and the *thermometer* to measure air temperature. They invented accurate *anemometers* to measure the speed of winds and *hygrometers* to measure moisture in the air. As they accumulated data from these new instruments, they discovered relationships between their measurements and future weather.

To accurately predict the weather, you need to measure the weather conditions at more than one place. You need to know what the weather conditions are over a wide area. (If the barometric pressure is falling in Philadelphia, you can guess that precipitation is on the way. However, only if you know that it is 20° F. (−7° C.) and snowing in Boston do you know that snow, rather than rain, is on the way.) Not until the telegraph became widespread in the late nineteenth century and a network of weather stations could send instant information over long distances could meteorologists predict the weather with accuracy.

13 Thermometer

The Problem

You are a scientist in Italy about 1590. You have seen that the hotness or coldness of liquids affects the way they behave. If hot water gets very hot, it turns to steam. If cold water gets very cold, it turns to ice. You have no system for measuring how hot "very hot" is and how cold "very cold" is, however. Wouldn't it be helpful if you could accurately measure the hotness or coldness of things? There are so many questions you could answer. . . .

Observations

In your laboratory, you often heat liquids in glass containers called *flasks*. Your flasks are *spherical,* meaning shaped like a ball, except that they have a narrow neck at the top, which can be closed with a cork. When you first started your experiments heating liquids, you made the mistake of putting a cork in the mouth of a flask. As the flask got hotter—Bam!—the cork flew off, across the room. You tried jamming the cork in very tightly, but then the flask itself exploded, sending glass and hot liquid everywhere. From hard experience, you've learned that heat makes something in the flask *expand* (get bigger).

MATERIALS

10-ounce (296-ml), empty, clean
  plastic soda bottle

transparent tape

ruler

pen

cork

adult helper

knife

nail

clear plastic straw

packing tape

water

food coloring

pan

Experiment

1. Put a piece of transparent tape on the soda bottle, from the top to the bottom. Using a ruler and a pen, mark the tape every ¼ inch (½ cm), and then number the marks from bottom to top.

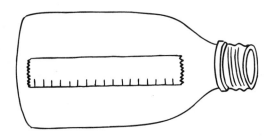

2. Make sure the cork will fit into the mouth of the bottle. Then have your adult helper cut the cork lengthwise. With the nail, scrape out a lengthwise channel down the center of each cork half, as shown.

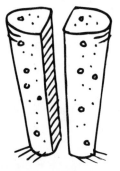

3. Fit the cork halves around the straw. Make sure that the straw will reach nearly to the bottom of the bottle when the cork is pushed into the top. Tape the two halves of the cork tightly together.

4. Fill the soda bottle about half full with cold water. Add a drop or two of food coloring. Push the cork into the mouth of the bottle. It should fit snugly. Note how high the water is in the straw, using the marks on the bottle.

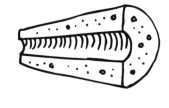

5. Put the bottle in the pan. Fill the pan with very hot water from the tap, so about one-third of the bottle is under water. Watch what happens to the water in the straw. It should rise as the water in the bottle absorbs the heat of the water in the pan. (If your tap water isn't hot enough, you may need to ask an adult to heat the water in the pan on the stove first, before you put the bottle in.) You've made a thermometer!

The hot water transfers energy to the molecules of nitrogen, oxygen, and other gases that make up air. As a result, the molecules in the air move faster and farther apart, which means the air in the bottle expands and takes up more space. In your experiment, when the air in the bottle expanded, it could not leave the bottle because of the cork, so it pushed down on the water at the bottom of the bottle. The only place the water could go was up the straw.

Answers from the Past

The ancient Greek philosophers noticed that heat makes air expand. Hero of Alexandria wrote about the phenomenon in the first century B.C. More than 1,500 years later, Galileo and his circle of friends in Italy began to explore the same phenomenon.

Galileo and other scientists of his day explored the natural world with what would become known as the **scientific method**. This was a method of research that involved taking precise measurements, making repeated experiments to test a **hypothesis** (a possible explanation of a set of facts), and drawing logical conclusions from data. When Galileo and his friends turned their attention to the way gases expand with heat, they wanted to do it in a scientific way.

In the mid-1590s, Galileo invented a device called a *thermoscope,* which demonstrated that heat makes air expand, and cooling makes it **contract** (occupy less space). (A **thermoscope** is a device that detects heat but doesn't measure heat in specific units as a **thermometer** does.) He took a tiny glass flask (about the size of a chicken egg) with a very long, strawlike neck and then warmed the flask in his hands. Then he turned the flask upside down and put the end of the neck in a bowl of water. When he took his hands away, the water rose up the neck of the flask.

Here's what happened in Galileo's device. When he warmed the flask, the air inside also became warmer. As it warmed, the gas molecules in the air moved more quickly and farther apart, and the air expanded. When he took his warm hands away, the air in the flask cooled. The gas molecules in the air moved more slowly and less far apart, so the air in the flask contracted. The water moved up the neck of the flask to take the place of the contracting air.

Other inventors in Europe developed similar thermoscopes at this time. Thermoscopes weren't particularly useful, however, because they did not measure specific temperatures. Some inventors tried marking a scale on their thermoscopes so that the changing temperature of the air could be measured. These were the first thermometers. Unfortunately, thermometers that depended on the expansion and contraction of air *(air thermometers)* were hard to use, and their measurements varied because they were affected by changes in air pressure. (See Chapter 14 on the barometer.)

About 1630, a French doctor named Jean Rey, realizing that liquids also expanded with heat, made the first liquid-in-glass thermometer, using alcohol as the liquid. Alcohol thermometers have a bulb at the bottom, filled with colored alcohol. The bulb opens into an extremely narrow, hollow tube inside a glass column. The tube in the glass column is so narrow that when the temperature rises a little and the alcohol in the bulb expands, it forces the alcohol level in the tube to rise dramatically. Alcohol thermometers could be much smaller than air thermometers.

In 1714, a German scientist and instrument maker named Daniel Gabriel Fahrenheit made a thermometer that used *mercury,* a metal that is liquid at room temperature. Mercury makes an excellent liquid for a thermometer because it doesn't cling to glass and therefore registers temperature very accurately. (Alcohol clings more to the glass than mercury does. On the other hand, mercury is a poison that can be absorbed through the skin, so it is a dangerous metal to work with.)

Fahrenheit also devised the first standard scale (called the **Fahrenheit scale**) for measuring temperature on his thermometer. Fahrenheit used the freezing temperature of salt water as his

0° point. On his scale, fresh water freezes at the 32° mark and boils at the 212° mark.

Anders Celsius, a Swedish astronomer, invented the **Celsius scale** for a thermometer in 1742. On the Celsius scale, fresh-water ice melts at 0°

Celsius originally labeled the scale with 0° as the boiling point of water and 100° as the melting point of ice! Thermometer makers soon reversed the order because people tend to think of warmer temperatures as being higher.

and boils at 100°. The Fahrenheit scale was commonly used in English-speaking countries until the 1970s, when the Celsius scale was generally adopted. Americans, however, still use the Fahrenheit scale.

Scientists around the world use the **Kelvin scale,** invented by William Thomson, Baron (Lord) Kelvin, in the late 1800s. Thomson, an Irish inventor and physics genius who went to college at the age of 10, invented a temperature scale that begins at absolute zero. **Absolute zero** (−460° F or −273° C) is the temperature at which the molecules of a substance would theoretically stop moving.

INVENTOR'S CHALLENGE

Potters' *kilns* (special high-temperature ovens) must be heated to temperatures between 1,000° and 3,500° F (550° and 2,000° C) to fire pots to hardness. The firing temperature is different for different clays. Potters can't use mercury thermometers to measure such high temperatures.

Ancient potters invented a different way of measuring heat. They would put a set of many **pyrometric** (meaning fire-measuring) clay cones into the kiln before heating up the oven. Each cone was made of a different clay known to melt at a particular temperature. When potters looked into the kiln, they could see how hot the kiln was by seeing which cones had melted.

Can you invent a similar kind of thermometer?

Materials

meat thermometer (an electronic one is best)

various food substances that could melt (such as butter, margarine, soft cheese, Crisco, Jell-O, a crayon, an old lipstick, a Lifesaver, chocolate)

metal baking pan

CLUES

Gather various materials that you guess might melt at relatively low temperatures. Put the samples in a metal baking pan, and put the pan in a sunny window, on top of a radiator, or in a sink of very hot water. Make a chart of their melting temperatures, as displayed on the meat thermometer.

14 Barometer

The Problem

You are a scientist in Italy in 1644. At this time, there are two great authorities on science: the ancient Greek philosopher Aristotle and the Catholic Church. According to these authorities, there are two facts related to air. One fact is that it is impossible to create a **vacuum** (a space with absolutely nothing in it) because air fills every space not occupied by solids or liquids. The second fact is that air has no weight.

You hesitate to challenge authority, but certain observations have made you and others believe that a vacuum is possible. Now, you question whether it is true that air has no weight. How can you prove that air has weight?

Observations

Last year, in 1643, your friend Gasparo Berti devised an experiment seeming to prove that the creation of a vacuum was possible. First, he attached a lead pipe more than 40 feet (12 meters) high to the wall of a tower. He submerged the bottom of the pipe, which had valves at both ends, in a barrel of water. Berti then closed the bottom valve and poured water down the pipe from the top until the pipe was full. Then he closed the top valve. Next, he opened the bottom valve. Some of the water (but far from all of it) came out of the bottom of the pipe, and the water level in the barrel rose slightly.

Everyone watching the experiment realized that Berti had created a vacuum at the top of the pipe. Water had come out of the bottom, and because the top valve was tightly closed, nothing could have taken its place. The space at the top of the pipe was completely empty.

When you open a glass bottle of juice next time, listen carefully. There is a vacuum between the bottle cap and the surface of the juice. When you take off the cap, you can hear the air rush in!

Berti's experiment convinced you that a vacuum can exist. Another piece of information from Berti's experiment now intrigues you. When Berti opened the valve at the bottom of the pipe, not all the water rushed out. What kept the water up in the pipe?

MATERIALS

clear jar, drinking glass, or plastic cup about 6 inches (15 cm) tall

6-inch (15-cm) plastic ruler (You can use a 12-inch (30-cm) ruler, but it's awkward.)

transparent tape

clear plastic drinking straw with a flexible accordion bend, about 8 inches (20 cm) long

water

a stick of chewing gum

pen

paper

Experiment

1. Stand the ruler inside the glass (or jar or cup). Tape the ruler to it.

2. Stand the straw inside the glass, next to the ruler. Make sure the bottom of the straw is ½ inch (1.25 cm) off the bottom of the glass. Tape the straw to the inside of the glass, next to the ruler.

3. Fill the glass about one third full with water.

4. Chew the chewing gum until it is soft. Keep the gum safely in the side of your mouth. Suck on the straw to draw some water half way up the straw. With your tongue, move the gum onto the top of the straw to seal it, so that the water does not fall back down. After the straw is sealed, the water level in the straw should be at least 1 inch (2.5 cm) above the surface of the water and at least 1 inch (2.5 cm) below the top of the ruler.

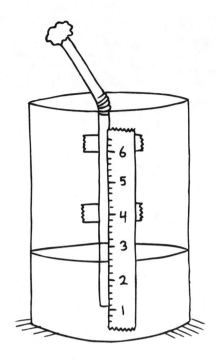

5. Note the level of water in the straw. Make a chart with four columns: (1) the date and time, (2) the water level in the straw, (3) the weather, and (4) the barometric pressure. (You can find the barometric pressure by looking at a barometer, calling your local weather service, or checking a weather service online.) Fill in the chart for the first day. Gather the same information every day for the next few weeks. Is there a relationship among the water level in the straw, the barometric pressure, and the weather?

Answers from the Past

In 1644, Evangelista Torricelli, an Italian scientist and friend of Galileo and Berti, realized that Berti's experiment proved not only that a vacuum can exist, but also that air has weight. If air didn't have weight, when Berti opened the bottom valve, all the water would have rushed down into the barrel. Instead, the weight of the air on the water in the barrel held up the water in the pipe.

Berti's experiment worked only because there was a vacuum at the top of the pipe. That meant there was no air pressing down on the water in the pipe. If the pipe had been open at the top, air would have pressed down on the water in the pipe. There would have been equal pressure on the water in and out of the pipe, so the water level inside the pipe and in the barrel would have been the same.

Air at sea level weighs about 14.7 pounds per square inch (1.02 kg per square cm). How can air weigh so much? Consider that Earth's atmosphere is more than 19 miles (30.4 km) high. That's a lot of air!

At this very moment, the pressure of air on you is equivalent to the weight of a car. Why aren't you crushed? The fluids inside your body also exert pressure, and the pressure of the air outside your body is balanced by the pressure of fluids inside.

Torricelli wanted to explore the weight of air (**air pressure**) further, but he realized that water was not a good liquid for further experiments. Water was not heavy enough: It took about 34 feet (10.5 meters) of water to balance approximately 19 miles (30.4 km) of air. Torricelli needed a heavier liquid than water, so that he wouldn't need to use so much of it. He decided to use mercury because it is much *denser* (it has a greater weight per volume) than water. In fact, a cup of mercury is about 14 times heavier than a cup of water.

In 1644, Torricelli took a glass tube sealed at the top end, filled it with mercury, removed most of the air from the tube, and put the open, bottom end into a bowl of mercury. The level of the mercury in Torricelli's tube—and in all mercury barometers—settled at about 30 inches (76 cm). Torricelli's device worked just as Berti's did, but it was a lot more practical to work with a 3-foot (1-meter) glass tube than a four-story lead pipe!

You created a miniature version of Berti's device. The air pressure on the surface of the water in the glass keeps the water in the tube from coming down. When you sucked on the straw in your experiment, you sucked most of the air out of it before you started to draw up the water. By removing the air and then sealing the top of the straw, you created a vacuum in the top of the straw. If there is air above the water in the straw when the barometric pressure rises, the water will not be able to rise as far because air already occupies the space.

Torricelli wrote to scientific colleagues in France about his invention. In 1647 and 1648, several French scientists and mathematicians, including René Descartes and Blaise Pascal, used Torricelli's device to explore questions about the weight of air. It appears that Descartes was the first to attach a scale to the device, which truly made it a **barometer** (a device to measure air pressure). Descartes, Pascal, and others confirmed that the weight of air changes with the weather.

Torricelli and others soon discovered that barometers could be used to predict the weather. A low reading signaled the arrival of rain or snow, and a high reading signaled the arrival of fair weather.

For a long time, no one knew why barometer readings changed before changes in the weather occurred. Now we know that moist air, which contains water vapor, is lighter than dry air. (It seems as though air with water in it should be heavier, but it's not so. The next time you take a hot shower, look at the mirror. You'll see that the mirror is steamed near the top and clears from bottom to top.) So when moist air is on the way, the mercury in the barometer falls. The light, moist air puts less pressure on the mercury, so it doesn't get pushed up as far in the barometer.

INVENTOR'S CHALLENGE

Use the following materials and your knowledge of air pressure to create what is known as an **aneroid** (using no fluid) barometer.

Materials
    empty coffee can
    plastic wrap
    rubber band
    2 straws
    tape
    pin
    ruler

CLUES
Fit one straw inside another, and tape them together. Tape the pin to one end to make an indicator.

15 Cup Anemometer

The Problem

You are an Irish scientist about 1840, and you are interested in studying the speed of the wind. You would like to be able to answer some questions, such as how much faster does the wind blow at higher altitudes, and what weather conditions produce stronger winds? The problem is that the device that you use to measure the speed of wind (called an **anemometer**) isn't accurate enough.

The best anemometers of the time look like miniature windmills. The wind pushes against the windmill's angled sails. As the sails turn, they turn a dial that measures the wind speed. The problem is that to keep the windmill anemometer facing the wind, it relies on another device attached to it— the **wind vane,** a device to show the wind's direction. If the windmill anemometer doesn't face into the wind, it doesn't measure the wind speed accurately. Unfortunately, the wind vane doesn't do a good job of keeping the anemometer facing into the wind when the winds are gusty and strong. There must be a better design. . . .

Observations

The *wind sock* is one of the world's oldest wind-sensing devices. It is made from fabric and has the shape of a funnel, with one wide open end and one narrow open end. A wire ring keeps the wide end open. A wind sock is hung from a pole by a wire attached to its wide end. As the wind enters the open end and fills out the sock, the sock rises and straightens out, pointing in the same direction as the wind is blowing. The stronger the wind, the closer the sock comes to being parallel to the ground.

A wind sock shows wind direction and gives people a rough idea of how strongly the wind is blowing. It doesn't give an accurate measurement of wind speed, though. The great advantage of the wind sock is that you don't have to make it face the wind, as you do the windmill anemometer. The wind turns the wind sock around the pole as it catches the open end of the sock. This makes you think. . . .

MATERIALS

five 3-ounce (88-ml) paper cups
hole punch
pencil with an eraser
two straight plastic soda straws
stapler
straight pin
modeling clay

Experiment

1. Use the hole punch to punch a hole in a paper cup, about ½ inch (1.25 cm) below the rim, as shown. Do the same for three more cups.

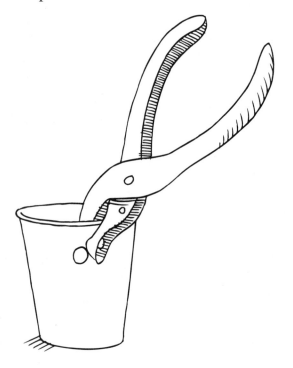

2. In the fifth cup, punch two holes about ¼ inch (0.6 cm) below the rim on opposite sides of the cup. Punch two more holes about ½ inch (1.25 cm) below the rim on opposite sides of the cup and halfway between the other two holes. Poke a hole in the bottom of this cup with your pencil, as shown.

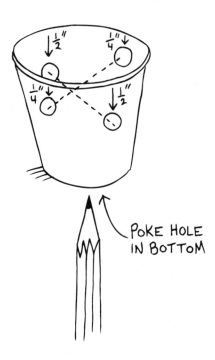

POKE HOLE IN BOTTOM

3. Take one of the one-hole cups, and push a straw all the way through the hole to the other side of the cup. Bend about ½ inch (1.25 cm) of the straw over, and staple the bent end to the side of the cup. Repeat this procedure for another straw and one-hole cup.

4. Take the five-hole cup. Push the free end of a straw from Step 3 through two opposite holes. Fit a one-hole cup on the other end of the straw, *facing the opposite way from the cup on the other end,* as shown. Bend the end of the straw over, and staple it as you did before. Repeat this procedure with the other cup and straw you assembled and with the last one-hole cup.

5. Now adjust the straws so that the cups' open ends all face the same way, as shown. Put a straight pin down through the two straws where they cross. Push the pencil, eraser end first, through the hole in the bottom of the five-hole cup and up to the pin. Push the pin into the eraser. You've made a cup anemometer! Push the pencil point into a mound of modeling clay, and hold the anemometer in front of a fan or in the wind.

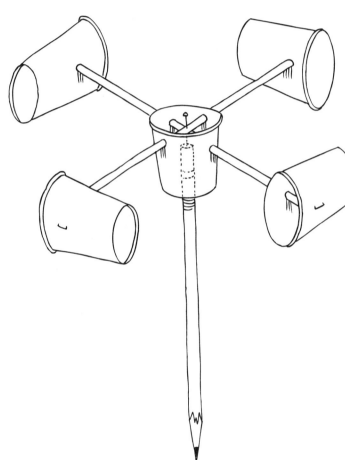

Answers from the Past

The first wind vanes were invented in ancient Greece. About 100 B.C., the Greeks built an octagonal marble tower that was crowned by a bronze statue of Triton (the half-man, half-fish demigod of the sea) holding a rod in his hand. The wind would catch Triton and his rod so that he always faced the wind.

> One wealthy ancient Greek farmer added a convenient feature to the wind vane. He had a wind vane built on his roof, which turned a pointer on the dining-room ceiling below, to show the wind's direction.

The first anemometer was invented about A.D. 1450. It was a wind vane with a swinging plate attached at the far end. The wind vane kept the plate perpendicular to the wind. The harder the wind blew, the farther up a curved scale the swinging plate would rise. The swinging-plate anemometer wasn't very accurate. Wind is often gusty, so the swinging plate moved up and down a lot, and it was hard to get a good measurement.

About 1700, a new kind of anemometer was invented. It looked like a windmill small enough to sit on a tabletop. (Windmills had been known throughout Europe since 1200.) The wind blew against the angled sails of the windmill, which turned a wheel. By measuring the rate at which the wheel turned, the wind speed was measured.

A big problem with both the swinging-plate anemometer and the windmill anemometer was that they had to face into the wind. Both of these anemometers used wind vanes to keep them turned to face the wind. Especially in high and shifting winds, though, wind vanes can be tossed from side to side. If wind vanes don't face the wind directly, then the attached anemometers can't measure the full force of the wind.

In 1846, an Irish scientist named Thomas Romney Robinson invented the **cup anemometer.** Its basic design was much like the paper-cup anemometer you built. (The cups in Robinson's anemometer, however, were hemispheres and turned a shaft that turned a wheel, which indicated its rate of rotation as the measure of the wind's speed.) Robinson's anemometer didn't need to face the wind. No matter what the direction of the wind, the rotating cups—like the wind sock—caught it. The cup anemometer was a big hit and soon replaced other kinds of anemometers of the day. The cup anemometer is still the standard design for anemometers around the world.

INVENTOR'S CHALLENGE

In 1775, James Lind invented another kind of anemometer. Lind's device used the changing water level in a bent tube to measure the wind's speed. Using the following materials, can you reinvent the water anemometer?

Materials

about 2 feet (60 cm) of plastic tubing (available at an aquarium supply or hardware store)
kitchen funnel
tape
lined index card
shoe box
water
hair dryer

CLUES

You will need to bend the tubing in several places. Use the shoe box to support the tubing. The hair dryer is just for creating a wind.

PART IV

Inventions to Live In

People have always needed to shelter themselves from the cold, rain and snow, and wild animals. Caves, when people could find them, made excellent shelters. There were many places, though, where humans lived, which had no caves, and people had to create their own shelters from materials they could find.

No doubt, people first made shelters from tree branches that they leaned against a rock or dirt cliff. They discovered that such a shelter would be sturdier if they wove slender branches or reeds together to make a kind of screen. Two screens leaned against each other could make a shelter when there was no cliff to hold up one screen. If there was mud around, the screens could be plastered with mud to make a more waterproof home. In hot, dry climates, mud alone—formed into bricks—made excellent houses.

It took creativity to build shelters in northern regions where there were no trees. In the northern regions of Europe and Russia, where people hunted herds of mammoths, they used the huge bones of their prey, packed with mud, to make homes. In the Arctic regions of North America and Greenland, people learned to make houses, as you will see, entirely from ice. People have experimented with shapes and materials for their homes for hundreds of thousands of years, and the inventing is far from over.

16 | Igloo

The Problem

You are an Inuit living near the ocean in northeastern Canada, thousands of years ago. You hunt caribou on land, and you fish in the sea in the summer. As winter approaches, your tribe must move south—your houses of sealskins spread over whalebones aren't strong or warm enough for the bitter cold winds of far northern winters.

The best seal hunting, though, is in winter. You can harpoon seals when they come up to breathe through holes in the ice. You would like to stay all winter to hunt them, but where will you live? What kind of shelter can you build to protect you from the even more bitter cold of the nights?

Observations

One of the animals you hunt is the polar bear. You have noticed that polar bears tunnel under the snow and make dens to sleep in. You have even stumbled upon a polar bear's abandoned den and crawled inside. Odd as it seems, you have found that snow can keep you warm.

You already know about cutting icy snow into blocks. Sometimes, while fishing at a hole in the ice, you have cut blocks of snow and piled them up into a wall to protect yourself from the winds that whip across the treeless tundra. It occurs to you that you could build a house of snow blocks to

keep warm. How should you build the house, though? What shape should it be? You know you can make walls out of snow, but what about a roof? Also, how can you hold the snow blocks together?

A snow shelter is surprisingly good at keeping people warm. After snow has fallen, a lot of air is trapped between the snowflakes. The air acts as **insulation**, keeping the cold outside separate from the warm inside. Snow works just the way a jacket filled with goose down (which is made of tiny feathers) does. Air gets trapped between the tiny feathery hairs of the down just the way air gets trapped between the tiny snowflakes in snow.

MATERIALS
butter knife

modeling clay (use white clay if you want to make your igloo look more realistic)

Experiment

1. Cut the modeling clay into about 36 identical bricks, roughly ½ × 1 × ¼ inches (1.25 × 2.5 × 0.6 cm). Stand the clay bricks on their long, thin edges, and build a house with four walls. Now cut some pieces of clay long enough to stretch from wall to wall as a roof. Put a little pressure on the roof. Did you discover a problem? Long slices of snow might not be such a good idea for a roof.

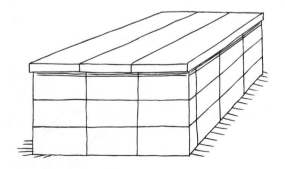

2. Take apart your house. Take 10 of your bricks, and push and stretch each one so that each is slightly trapezoidal. (A **trapezoid** is a four-sided figure that has two parallel and two nonparallel sides, as shown.) Start building a wall with these bricks, but as you build the wall, bend each brick a little so that it is slightly curved, as shown. Build until you have formed a circular wall.

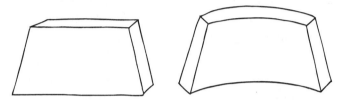

3. With your knife, slice diagonally through the first 2 bricks in your wall. Take 10 more of your bricks, and push and stretch them so they are trapezoidal. Start the next row of bricks going up the slope created by the diagonal cut. Lay the bricks in a spiral up and around, as shown. As you put on each additional brick, you will find you need to make the angles at the base of the trapezoid a little sharper because the spiral will get tighter and tighter.

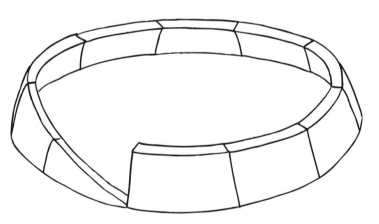

4. At the top, there will be a hole. Cut a brick to fill the hole, as shown. Push down gently on your structure. Is it sturdy? You've made an igloo!

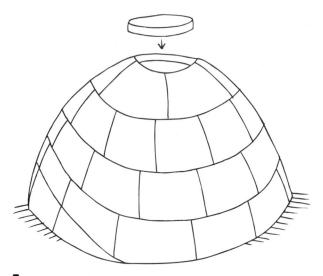

Answers from the Past

The **igloo** (which comes from the Inuit word *iglu*, meaning any kind of house) was invented by people who lived in northeastern Canada about 2,000 to 3,000 years ago. Although few people live in igloos anymore, without this wonderful snow house, life in many parts of the far north would have been impossible.

To make an igloo, the Inuit first had to search for snow of just the right consistency. Too soft, and the blocks would fall apart. Too hard, and the snow would be too difficult to cut. The Inuits built their igloos on a slope if at all possible, with the entrance facing down the slope and to the south, so the igloo was sheltered from the northern winds.

The igloo builder would cut blocks of snow from a trench just in front of where the igloo would be. Each block was cut in a slightly trapezoidal shape, just like the blocks you just made out of clay. Like you, the builder would arrange the blocks in a circle and then slice a slope through the first two. The builder would cut all the rest of the blocks from inside the igloo floor and place them, one after another, in a continuing, upward-spiraling wall. The last, topmost block was placed from the outside.

After placing each block, the igloo builder would slide the knife up and down between the blocks. The friction of the knife rubbing against the snow melted the snow blocks a little. When they refroze, they stuck together in a solid bond.

Igloos were so strong that they could take the weight of a person sitting on top. (Inuit children would play games and slide down the sides of their snow houses.) Igloos varied in size, but a typical igloo for a family of four or five was between 9 and 12 feet (3 and 4 meters) in diameter (which is less than twice the length of your bed) and 8 feet (2½ meters) tall in the center. The Inuit usually put a window in their igloo. The window was made of a block of clear, fresh-water ice or from a piece of seal gut.

How did people stay warm in an igloo? Each family had a soapstone bowl that the family would fill with seal blubber as fuel, which would be burned, to use as a stove. The heat of these small stoves, along with body heat, kept the inside of the igloo at about 55° F (13° C.).

Igloos had a tunnel entrance that sloped down and away from the igloo itself. Because cold air is heavier than warm air, cooling air in the igloo would head down the tunnel, away from the people.

Igloos also had a very small ventilation hole at the top and several such holes at floor level. Hot, stale air rose out the top hole and pulled a little fresh air in through the floor-level holes. The cold fresh air mixed instantly with the warmer air inside, freshening it without overly chilling it.

The shape and construction of the igloo were perfect for the environment. The walls were **translucent** (letting light through). This was important in the far north where, during the winter, there would be only a few hours of daylight at most. Also, when the wind blew, the dome shape offered less resistance to the air than would a house with flat walls. The wind could flow around an igloo instead of knocking it down. Because winds blow down, as well as across, the pressure on the top of the dome actually strengthened the igloo, packing the blocks of snow more tightly together.

INVENTOR'S CHALLENGE

If your building material happens to be packed snow, you can make an excellent domed shelter in the way that the Inuits did. The Inuits could easily cut each snow block to the exact shape needed. As they built an igloo's circular, spiraling wall, they changed the shape of the blocks so that the wall formed a dome. You did the same thing with your clay blocks when you built your clay igloo.

Snow can be molded easily, but what if your building materials are stone or brick of a few standard sizes? Can you still build a dome? See whether you can invent a domed structure made out of clay shaped into rectangular bricks. (Don't bend the clay rectangles when you build—remember, the rectangles represent unbendable stone or brick.) Try triangular and **pentagonal** (five-sided) bricks. See which of your buildings is the most stable and looks the most dome-like.

Materials
modeling clay

17 Tilted Tipi

The Problem

It is about 1650, and you are a member of the Sioux tribe. Your tribe has lost a long war with the neighboring Ojibwa. (The Ojibwa finally won with guns they got in trade for furs with French trappers.) As a result, your people have been forced to flee south, away from your homes, along the wooded shores of what is now called Lake Superior and into the great grass plains of what is now North and South Dakota.

You have left a whole way of life behind. No longer can you live by harvesting the wild rice that grows by the lake shores and by spearing fish from your bark canoes. Now, you must hunt the migrating herds of buffalo for food. Fortunately, the buffalo are plentiful, and from horseback, they are not difficult to kill.

You used to live in **wigwams** built of wood cut from many *saplings* (young, flexible trees), shaped into a dome, and covered in bark or reed mats. Here on the plains, though, there are few trees and no reeds. Other tribes who cross the prairie following the buffalo—the Cheyenne, the Comanche, and the Crow—live in cone-shaped tents made of long poles tied at the top and covered with buffalo skins stitched together. You call these **tipis** and learn how to make them.

Tipis are lightweight and easy to take apart, which is essential because you are constantly traveling as you follow the herds. The big problem with tipis is that they're smoky. Smoke from the fires you build for heating and cooking gets trapped in the tipi. How can you solve this problem?

Observations

The smoke goes out through the small hole at the top of the cone-shaped tipi where the poles are lashed together. Small holes don't let out all of the smoke, however. Unfortunately, if you made the hole at the top large enough to let out all the smoke, it would also be large enough to let rain and snow in. It would be best if you could adjust the size of the smoke hole, depending on the weather and the size of your fire, but that's impossible to do, given the way this tipi is designed.

MATERIALS

Experiment A
  modeling clay
  18 coffee stirrers

Experiment B
  copier paper (or typing paper or notebook paper)
  scissors
  tape
  pencil
  five 8-inch (20-cm) bamboo skewers (available at grocery stores)
  paper-covered wire ties

Experiment A

1. Form the clay into 12 balls about the size of large peas.

2. Form a triangle with three stirrers, using the balls of clay to hold the corners together. Then add three more stirrers and one more clay ball to the triangle to form a pyramid, as shown.

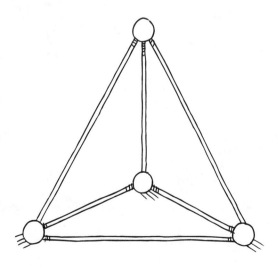

3. Form a square with four balls and four stirrers. Use the rest of the balls and stirrers to make the square into a cube, as shown.

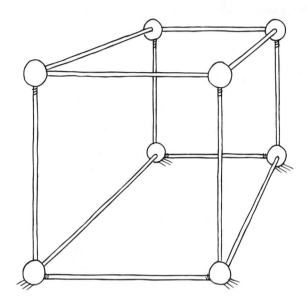

4. Experiment with putting gentle pressure on the top and on the sides of each structure. Which one stands up to your pressure better?

Triangles are good at resisting pressure. As you can see from this experiment, a three-dimensional structure made of triangles is also sturdy. Because a cone is based on a triangle, it is also sturdy. Many early tribes around the globe figured out that a cone shape is strong, and they built conical homes from a variety of materials.

Experiment B

1. Make two copies of the Tipi Cover Pattern (see p. 73) in a copier, or trace it onto paper. Cut out the copies along the solid edges. Turn one copy upside down, and slide it over the other copy so that the dotted lines labeled A overlap. Both arrows should point in the same direction. Tape the copies together. Put the paper (your tipi cover) on a table, and crease the paper along the dotted lines labeled B so that both flaps point up at you. You are looking at the outside of your tipi cover (which you can decorate if you like).

2. Bend the cover into a cone shape so the edges meet at C and D, and the flaps are on the outside. Tape the edges of the tipi cover together at C and D. The circular opening is the tipi entrance, and the flaps are the tipi's smoke flaps.

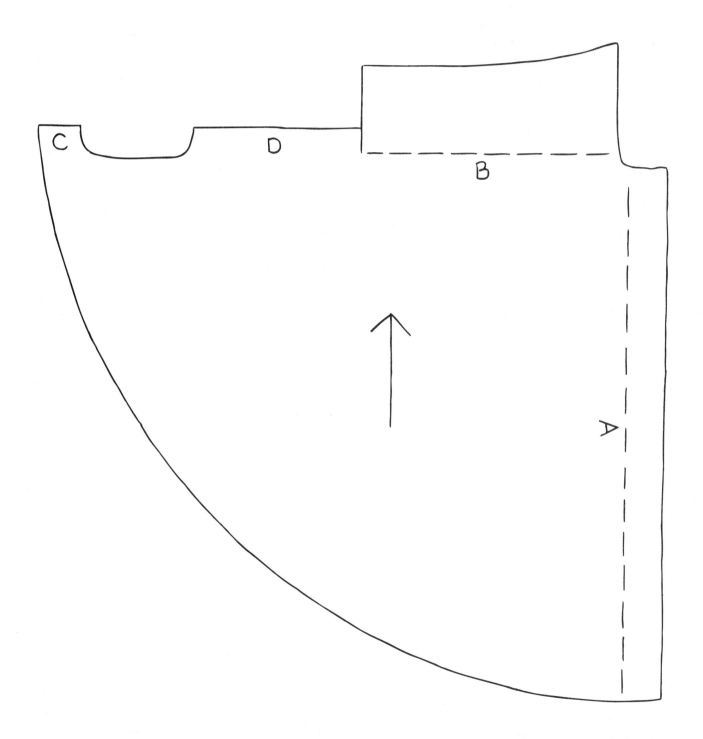

3. Stand three of the skewers on their points in a tripod shape so that they cross at about 5½ inches (14 cm) up the skewers. Wrap a tie around the three skewers where they meet, as shown.

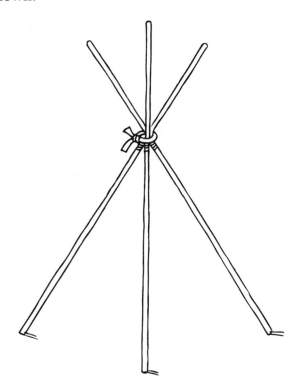

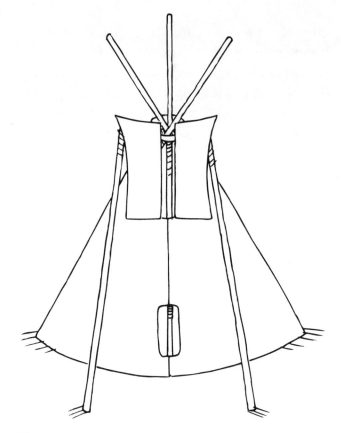

4. Place the tipi cover over the cone of skewers (the tipi frame). Adjust the shape of the frame to fit the tipi cover.

5. Take the remaining two skewers, and tape the tip of one skewer to the top corner of each smoke flap, so that the other end rests on the ground.

6. You've made a tilted tipi, much as the Sioux made them! Use the poles on the smoke flaps to open and close their top edges.

f you look at this tipi from the side you will notice that it is tilted. The front seam of the tipi is longer than the back seam. The Sioux (and other Plains Indians) would place the tipi's hearth so that it was directly below the smoke flaps instead of below the peak of the tipi.

This innovative design for a conical home made the tilted tipi a much more comfortable structure to live in than a regular tipi. The top corners of the smoke flaps were attached to long poles, which were used to adjust the position of the flaps. The flaps could be closed to shelter the smoke hole to keep rain or snow out while letting smoke escape. They could be opened for large fires to let more smoke out.

Tilted tipis were well ventilated. The hot air rising from the fire would draw cool, fresh air in from the entrance and from under the edges of the tipi. The smoke rose directly up from the fire and out through the smoke hole.

Answers from the Past

For many thousands of years, people around the world, including Native Americans, placed bark, reed mats, and skins around branches or poles arranged in a cone shape to make homes. All these dwellings let the smoke from their fires escape through the hole centering around the crossed poles at the top. No one can say for certain who developed the tilted tipi or when, but it could have been the Sioux, in the middle of the seventeenth century, who perfected the design.

The Sioux started a tipi frame with 3 poles, as you started yours with 3 skewers. The Sioux, however, added about 9 to 12 poles to the first 3 to complete a frame. In most tribes, the women made the tipis and erected them. They cut buffalo skins into strips, stitched them together into a rectangular shape, and then cut the rectangle into the roughly semicircular shape of the tipi cover. The edges of the cover in front were held together with leather laces. Many of the tipis had an inner lining for warmth.

Because tipis are made from perishable skins and wood, the early ones have not survived. Because the tribes had no written language at the time, they left no written records that might help us discover the tipi's origins.

As the use of the horse spread throughout tribes in the American West in the eighteenth century, so did the use of tipis. It was much easier for a horse than for a dog to drag the long tipi poles from one campground to the next. After hunters killed nearly all the buffalo during the late nineteenth century, Native Americans had to use canvas for their tipi covers. Because canvas is lighter than buffalo hides, tipis could be much larger. Some were 30 feet (over 9 meters) wide and taller than a four-story building.

During the first decades of the twentieth century, most Native Americans stopped living in tipis. Yet still during the summer months, when tribes gather for ceremonies and to socialize, they often pitch tipis to make sure that this great technology isn't lost.

INVENTOR'S CHALLENGE

People who lived 15,000 years ago on the cold and windy steppes of Ice Age Europe had no trees with which to make shelters. The only building materials were mammoth bones, stones, and mud. Use the following materials to build a model of a shelter for these Ice Age humans.

Materials
gravel
8-inch (24-cm) bamboo skewers broken in half (miniature mammoth bones)
Play-Doh or modeling clay (mud)

[18] Geodesic Dome

The Problem

It is the late 1940s, and you are an American inventor and amateur architect. You are deeply concerned about the shortage of housing in America and around the world. Too many people, you believe, go without adequate housing because supplies of wood are dwindling, and the costs of wood, brick, and metal are rising. You would like to develop a new design for houses that would use fewer materials and be cheaper to build, but still be sturdy and comfortable.

Observations

One day in kindergarten, your teacher gives every child in the class a bunch of half-dried peas and a bundle of toothpicks. She tells everybody to make a building by connecting the peas with the toothpicks. The other kids make buildings with rectangular and square walls, roofs, and floors, just like the houses they live in and the barns they see. Your buildings are different. You make yours of triangles. You know, without anyone teaching you, that triangular shapes are the most stable shapes.

Later, you study geometry and learn that a sphere encloses a given amount of space with the least amount of material.

MATERIALS
copier or printer paper
pencil
8 or more unlined index cards
transparent tape
ruler
scissors

Experiments

1. Trace or copy the Triangle A Pattern below onto copier paper, and cut it out. Note that it is an **equilateral** triangle, meaning that all its sides are the same length, and the angles where the sides meet (the **vertices**) are the same. Each angle in an equilateral triangle is 60°.

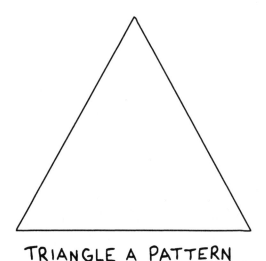

TRIANGLE A PATTERN

2. Using the Triangle A Pattern, make 20 exact copies of it, either by tracing on index cards or by copying on a photocopier.

3. On each triangle, draw three lines that will divide the triangle into three smaller triangles, as shown. First, find the middle of a side and make a mark. Then draw a line from that mark to the tip of the point opposite that side. Do the same for each of the other two sides and points.

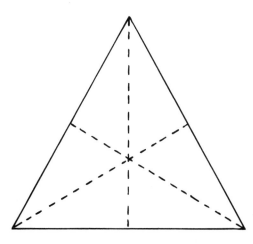

4. An **icosahedron** is a solid made of 20 equilateral triangles. Look at the drawing of an icosahedron. Using small pieces of tape to attach the triangles, see whether you can tape your triangles together to make an icosahedron. (Hint: To start, tape five triangles together.)

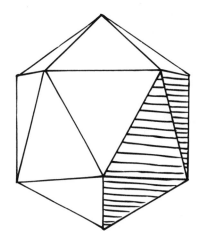

5. Notice how the triangles fit together into **pentagons** (five-sided shapes). Take one of the pentagons off your icosahedron, as shown. Stand your icosahedron on its open edges. You've made your first geodesic dome!

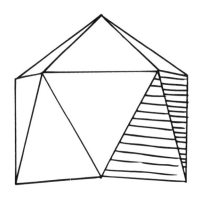

A **geodesic dome** is a network of triangles linked together to form part of a sphere. *Geodesic* means earth-dividing. The equator around a globe is a geodesic line—it divides the sphere into hemispheres.

6. Imagine increasing the size of your dome so that you could stand up in it. Wouldn't it be a more comfortable place if you could push out on the middle of those flat triangles (where your pencil lines cross) to give you a little more room? You can. Trace or copy the Triangle B Pattern below 20 times onto copier paper. Cut out the pattern along the solid edges. Crease the shape along the dotted edges. Tape the edges together to form a pyramid shape.

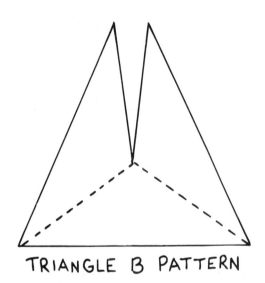

TRIANGLE B PATTERN

7. Tape a pyramid cap onto each triangular face of your icosahedron. Imagine then removing all the triangles underneath. By using pyramids instead of flat triangles, you can increase the area inside your dome.

Answers from the Past

Late one cold night in 1927, a 32-year-old American named Richard Buckminster Fuller stood on the shore of Lake Michigan. He was depressed beyond words. The last several years of his life had been full of losses. His 4-year-old daughter, Alexandra, had died after a series of illnesses. He had lost two jobs, he was nearly penniless, and he felt like an utter failure. Looking out over the water, he contemplated swimming out "until I became exhausted and sank."

Fuller didn't do that, though. Instead, he decided to reorient his life and to dedicate him-self to bettering the condition of humanity. He knew that people around America and around the world needed better housing. He decided he would use his knowledge and imagination to invent a house that would cost less to build.

In short order, Fuller dreamed up a single-story, flat-roofed, hexagonal house made of a thin metal skin and hung from a pole. He couldn't make the house work, though, because a material that would make a thin metal skin so large hadn't been invented yet. (If this house were built today, a builder would use sheets of aluminum.) In 1940, he invented a house made from steel grain-storage bins. (The U.S. military bought them as houses for defense workers.) Then, in the late 1940s, Fuller began to study the geometry of spheres.

Fuller knew that a sphere was the most efficient shape for enclosing any particular amount of space. Fuller also knew that a sphere made up of triangles would be sturdy because triangles are the most rigid shape. He reasoned that domes made of triangles would make strong, low-cost homes.

To picture the difference between a dome-shaped house and a box-shaped house, think about this: If your bedroom contained 800 cubic feet (246 cubic meters) of space in a cube shape, and you wanted to paint the walls, ceiling, and floor, you'd have to paint 519 square feet (160 square meters). If your room contained the same 800 cubic feet, but was spherical, you'd only have to paint 415 square feet (128 square meters).

Fuller built hundreds of models of domes of all sizes, shapes, and materials before he got his first purchase order. In 1953, Ford Motor Company wanted to cover the huge, round courtyard in the middle of one of its buildings in Michigan. The space was so large it couldn't be covered with traditional materials: The weight of traditional roof materials (160 tons) would collapse the supporting walls. Ford hired Fuller to do the job. He designed a dome that weighed only 8.5 tons. It was made of thousands of aluminum triangles, and it worked perfectly.

Fuller's geodesic domes have covered stadiums, concert halls, greenhouses, and radar stations near the Arctic Circle. Fuller and his wife lived for years in a plywood dome. Domes, though, haven't become humankind's solution to the problem of affordable housing. For one thing, with all the joints between triangles, they're hard to waterproof. It's also hard to partition a dome into rooms. Still, there are thousands of geodesic domes around the world in use as small homes and as public buildings.

INVENTOR'S CHALLENGE

Using some or all of the following materials, find a new shape for a house. Can you make separate rooms inside? Remember that a house needs doors, windows, and stairs.

Materials

clear lids from plastic deli containers
bamboo skewers or pencils
modeling clay
clear packing tape
posterboard
scissors
colored markers

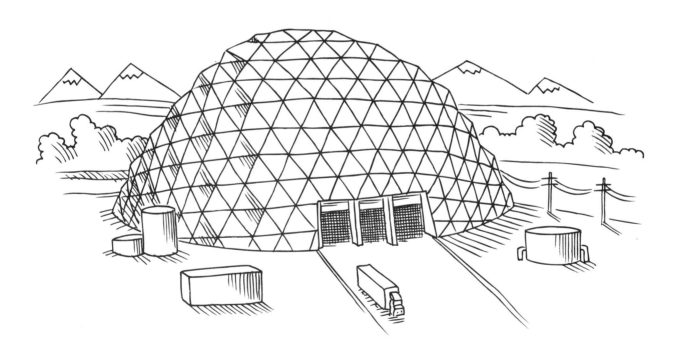

PART V

Inventions That Use Magnetism and Electricity

About 2,300 years ago, the ancient Chinese discovered that a piece of a certain kind of stone—what we know as **lodestone**—always aligned itself in a particular direction. With this observation, the Chinese invented the first magnetic compasses. We know now that lodestone acts like a magnet and aligns with Earth's magnetic field to point north and south.

About 2,000 years ago, a Greek philosopher named Thales discovered that he could produce sparks by rubbing a cloth against a clear, yellow substance called amber. In the mid-1700s, a Dutch scientist named Pieter van Musschenbroek discovered a way to store those friction-created sparks—what we call static electricity—in a jar. In 1800, Alessandro Volta invented a device, the wet-cell battery, that generated electricity through chemical changes, rather than friction.

By the nineteenth century, many scientists had come to believe there was a connection between magnetism and electricity, and their experiments proved it. In 1820, a Danish scientist named Hans Ørsted discovered that a wire carrying an electrical current acted as a magnet. Eleven years later, in 1831, English experimenter Michael Faraday discovered that when a magnet was pushed in and out of a wire coil, it generated electricity.

By the end of the century, American inventors were using their understanding of the relationship between magnetism and electricity to invent dozens of new devices. Thomas Davenport invented a direct-current motor in 1837, Samuel Morse tested the electric telegraph in 1844, Alexander Graham Bell invented the telephone in 1876, Thomas Edison developed electric lightbulbs in the 1880s, and Nikola Tesla invented the alternating-current motor (the basis of most modern motors) in 1883. You'll learn more about several of these inventions in this part of the book.

[19] Marine Compass

The Problem

You are a fisher out on the ocean off the coast of China in A.D. 850, and you are nervous. The fish are running far from shore, and you have to leave sight of land this morning to catch them. Dark gray clouds obscure the sun now and will hide the stars tonight. Without the sun or stars to help you navigate, it will be hard to find your way back home. If only there were another way to figure out your direction. . . .

Observation

You have watched the magicians in your village many times as they helped people decide exactly how to build a new house. (Everyone in your village knows you will have bad luck unless you properly align a new house with Earth's breaths that come from the north, south, east, and west.) The magicians use what is called a *south-pointer*, a device that always points south and, therefore, shows where all the other directions are. A south-pointer consists of a needle that has been rubbed with a special stone and then hung from a silk thread inside a cup.

A south-pointer would help point the way home when you couldn't see the sun or stars. Unfortunately, your boat tosses and turns so, the delicate south-pointer would never work. You see a piece of bark floating by, and it gives you an idea. . . .

MATERIALS

compass
2 bar magnets
sewing needle
thread
scissors
pencil
tall drinking glass
small bowl
water
slice of cork (have an adult cut this) or a piece
    the size of a quarter cut from the bottom of a
    Styrofoam cup
glue

Experiments

1. First, look at your compass, and turn it so the "N" (for north) is directly under the compass needle.

2. Experiment with your bar magnets by holding them next to each other in different ways. Notice how each magnet has an end *(pole)* that either pulls the other magnet toward it or pushes it away. (Caution: Be sure not to get the magnets too close to the compass because they can ruin the compass magnet.)

> **B**ar magnets contain iron, and iron—as you will see—can be magnetized. Every magnet has two ends, or **poles**. In your experiments, you will see that the north end of one bar magnet attracts the south end of the other. Two north ends and two south ends repel each other.

3. Hold your sewing needle near its middle. Take a bar magnet and point the north end (marked "N") at the needle. Stroke the north end of the magnet along the needle from the middle of the needle to the end with the eye

in it, then lift the magnet away. Do this 50 times. Then, use the south end of the magnet to stroke the other half of the needle from the middle to the sharp point, 50 times. Make sure you always lift the magnet away from the needle after each stroke.

4. Cut a piece of thread about 6 inches (15 cm) long. Tie one end around the middle of the needle. Tie the other end around the middle of a pencil. Place the pencil across the top of the glass. The needle should be able to turn without hitting the sides of the glass. (You may need to shorten the thread.) When the needle stops turning, compare where it points to the direction of the compass needle. The eye of the needle in the glass will be pointing north. You've made an ancient Chinese magician's compass!

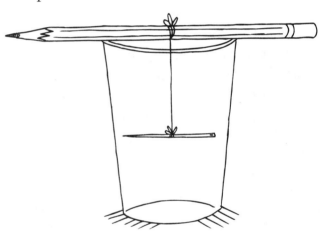

> **W**hy does the needle point to the north? Earth itself acts as a huge bar magnet because it has a magnetized iron core. Like your magnets, Earth has a north and a south pole. The north and south poles attract each other, causing lines of magnetic force running between the two poles. Magnetic compass needles point north and south because they line up in these lines of magnetic force.

5. Fill the bowl full of water. Place your magnetized needle on the slice of cork or piece of Styrofoam. Put one drop of glue on the needle to secure it to the cork. When the glue dries, float the cork and needle in the middle of the bowl of water. Compare it to the compass. The pointed end should point south. You've made an ancient Chinese marine compass!

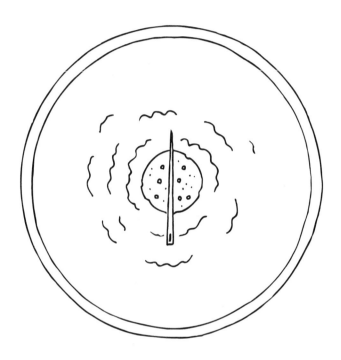

6. Pick up the bowl. Tilt and turn it. What happens to the water and compass? Does tilting the bowl affect how the compass works?

Answers from the Past

In ancient China, magicians believed they could foretell the future by playing a kind of game. They took five small objects—standing for air, wood, fire, metal, and water—and tossed them on a board. Then they would predict the future based on the positions of the pieces relative to each other. One day, probably in the fourth century B.C., a magician tossed a stone piece shaped like a spoon and noticed something curious. No matter how he tossed the spoon, it always turned on its bowl and pointed north.

The spoon turned toward the north, people soon realized, only when it was made out of *tzu shih*, the "loving stone." The loving stone earned its name because it attracted bits of iron to it. We now know that loving stone, which we call *lodestone*, attracts iron because it is naturally magnetic. The spoon was essentially a bar magnet that aligned itself with earth's magnetic forces. For centuries the Chinese used a lodestone spoon balanced on a plate as a compass.

> The ancient Chinese had no understanding of magnetism and what made lodestone spoons point toward north. They guessed that the spoons were afraid of the south. The ancient Chinese associated heat and fire with the south and therefore assumed that the spoons were afraid of heat that might melt them.

By about A.D. 650, Chinese magicians had learned to rub a lodestone against an iron needle so that the needle became magnetized. They made compasses (south-pointers) much like yours, using a silk thread and a cup. Compasses were used to position houses in the most favorable way and to help people find their way on land.

Possibly as early as A.D. 850, the Chinese had developed a compass that could be used on boats at sea. (The Europeans and the Arabs didn't develop a marine compass until about 1200.) The compass used a floating needle and a piece of bark, much like the one you made. It worked on a boat because even if the boat tilted, the water in the bowl stayed horizontal, and the needle still turned freely.

For thousands of years before the compass, people relied on two celestial phenomena to identify north, south, east, and west: the sun and the North Star. They knew the sun always rises in the east and sets in the west (although the sun's exact position changes with the season). They also used the North Star—the one directly above the last two stars in the Big Dipper constellation—to identify north at night. The compass was a major advance because it allowed sailors to explore farther and farther from shore without fear of losing their way.

INVENTOR'S CHALLENGE

Can you invent a magnetic game using some or all of the following materials? Try one that challenges a single player's *manual dexterity* (skill in the use of the hands) and another that involves a competition between two players.

Materials

    disk magnets
    bar magnets
    sheet of cardboard
    paper clips
    modeling clay
    posterboard
    scissors
    pencils
    tape

CLUES

Can magnetic force pass through cardboard? Remember how like ends of magnets repel each other. The cardboard sheet has possibilities both when flat and when tilted.

20 | Leyden Jar

The Problem

It is 1746, and you are a professor of mathematics and physics at the University of Leyden in the Netherlands. Ever since 1663, when German scientist Otto von Guericke invented a machine capable of generating electricity through friction, scientists—as well as ordinary citizens—have been fascinated by electricity. Scientists and showpeople in Europe and America have invented a variety of static-electricity devices that make glass globes glow and cause bright blue sparks

to shoot through the air. One experimenter in Germany hung a small boy by a silk harness and put the boy's feet onto a turning glass globe. Then he drew sparks from the boy's nose!

The problem, though, is that no one can store this electricity. If you want to produce a spark or make an object attract paper, you have to crank a machine to do it. Shortly after you stop cranking, though, the electrical charge disappears. It would be helpful if you could somehow save the charge, so you could use it later—but how?

The ancient Greeks knew that if you rubbed *amber* (a fossilized yellow resin from trees) with a cloth, it would attract bits of dust and straw. By the seventeenth century, scientists realized there were two kinds of electricity (what we call positive and negative charge). Rubbing amber created one kind of charge, and rubbing glass produced the other. Straw that was attracted by rubbed amber would be repulsed by rubbed glass.

Guericke invented a machine that provided continuous friction and therefore a constant electrical charge to an object. Guericke's device consisted of a big sulfur ball on an iron rod. When Guericke turned the ball (first by hand and later by crank) and let a rod rub across the surface, the ball and the rod became oppositely charged. After a short amount of time, though, the ball and rod lost their charge.

Observations

You've spent a lot of time experimenting with Guericke's machines. One day, you experiment with the device, a copper wire, and a jar of water. The result of this experiment was shocking. . . .

MATERIALS

Experiment A
   plastic or hard-rubber comb
   clean cotton cloth
   small bits of scrap paper

Experiment B
   plastic 35-mm film canister
   2-inch (5-cm) nail
   aluminum foil
   scissors
   tape
   water
   measuring spoons
   salt
   TV
   adult helper

Experiment A

1. Rub the comb vigorously with the cloth.

2. Hold the comb near the small bits of paper. What happens? (The paper should jump to the comb.) How long do the pieces of paper stick? If you had a machine (like Guericke's device) that would rub the cloth continuously on the comb, the paper would stay there as long as the machine was running.

Experiment B

1. Take the top off of the film canister. Push the pointed end of the nail through the top from above. Leave the head and about ⅓ inch (1 cm) of the nail sticking out the top.

2. Cut a strip of foil 4½ inches (11½ cm) wide and long enough to go around the canister. Wrap it tightly around the outside of the bottom two thirds of the canister. Tape it in place securely, but make sure the tape doesn't cover all the foil.

Materials are made up of invisible particles called atoms. *Atoms* are made of even smaller particles called protons, neutrons, and electrons. Before you rubbed the comb, the atoms that made up the comb were electrically neutral. That means the comb's atoms had an equal number of **protons**, which carry a positive (+) charge, and **electrons**, which carry a negative charge (-). (**Neutrons** have no charge; they are neutral.)

When you rubbed the comb, you stripped away electrons from atoms in the cloth and transferred them to the comb. The comb became negatively charged because it then had more negative electrons than positive protons. (The comb had **static electricity**. An object has static electricity when it carries a charge—an excess of positively or negatively charged particles—and the charge does not flow beyond the object.) When the negatively charged comb approached the bits of paper, it attracted positively charged atoms in the paper. Eventually, the comb attracts enough positive charge to balance its negative charge, and the comb becomes electrically neutral again. Even if there is no paper around, the comb would attract tiny particles in the air and would become neutral again.

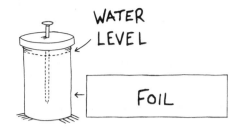

WATER
LEVEL

FOIL

3. Fill the canister nearly full of water, add ¼ teaspoon (1 ml) of salt, put the cap on, and shake it.

4. Cut a square of aluminum foil smaller than your TV's screen. Tape it to the glass of the screen with a few small pieces of tape. Lift one corner of the foil, and bend it toward you, as shown.

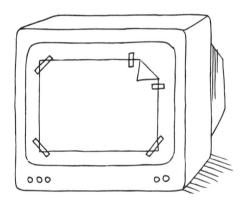

5. Turn the TV on. Hold the canister by the foil, and quickly bring the nail head up to the bent corner of foil on the TV. You may be able to see sparks of electricity jump from the TV to the nail, especially if the room is dark. Hold the canister to the foil for a few seconds.

6. Was the electricity from the TV stored in your Leyden jar? Hold the canister by the foil with one hand, and touch the nail with the other hand to find out!

How does your Leyden jar work? Inside a TV, there is a gun that shoots electrons at the inside of a large, glass TV tube coated with a **fluorescent** (capable of emitting light) material. Most of the electrons are stopped by the tube, where they make the picture that glows on the TV screen. Some electrons, however, pass through the tube into the room. In your experiment, the aluminum foil that you taped onto the screen collects those electrons, making the foil negatively charged.

When you touch the nail head of your Leyden jar to the negatively charged foil on the TV, the electrons flow into the nail because metal is a good **conductor** (carrier) of electricity. The nail becomes negatively charged and generates a negative **electric field**. (An electric field extends through space from charged particles and exerts a force on other charged particles.) Electrons in the foil taped to the canister are repelled by the nail's negative electric field and move to the outer surface of the foil.

Because you are holding the canister by the foil, the electrons continue to move away from the nail, through your body to the ground. This process (called **grounding**) happens because Earth is a large and extremely good conductor of electric charge. As the electrons leave the foil, the amount of positive charge left on the foil exceeds the amount of negative charge, so the foil becomes positively charged. Physicists call this method of creating an electrical charge in an object **induction by grounding**.

Your Leyden jar is now charged. The foil on the outer surface has a positive charge. The nail on the inside has a negative charge. The two charges are separated by the plastic of the canister, which is a good **insulator**.

In the last step of the experiment, you bring your free hand to the nail head. You then become a pathway for the electrons on the nail to flow toward the positively charged foil. The electrons flow from the nail through your fingertip through your body to the foil. You feel the flow as a static shock. In the dark, you may see the spark of electricity. Fortunately, the jar holds only a small amount of charge, so you get a very mild shock.

Answers from the Past

One day in the lab, while experimenting with one of Guericke's devices, Pieter van Musschenbroek held one end of a copper wire near the turning, charged ball and put the other end in a jar of water. His assistant, Cunaeus, held the jar. Musschenbroek cranked the device as fast as he could, but it didn't seem to be working. He stopped turning the crank, and Cunaeus, still holding the jar, reached out to touch the wire to see what the problem was. Suddenly, zap! A spark cracked in the air, and Cunaeus tumbled backward.

Musschenbroek understood that somehow he had stored electricity and that his assistant suddenly released that electricity by creating a path for it to flow out. What Musschenbroek didn't understand was where the electricity was stored. He thought it was in the water. (Actually, it was in the wire and the outside of the jar.) That was because scientists at the time thought electricity was a weightless, invisible fluid.

Musschenbroek's device became known as the Leyden jar because Musschenbroek lived in the city of Leyden (sometimes spelled "Leiden"). The early Leyden jars were water-filled glass jars that were stoppered with a cork pierced by a nail. In 1747, English physician and scientist William Watson refined the jar by eliminating the water and instead lining the inside and outside of the glass with metal foil. The nail touched the foil on the inside, so the foil became electrically charged. Watson was able to transmit a spark from his Leyden jar through a wire strung across the Thames River in London.

Leyden jars were a great help in making further experiments in electricity because electricity could be stored in them for a period of time. Experimenters were able to ignite alcohol, light candles, and explode gunpowder with electricity stored in a Leyden jar.

Ben Franklin used a Leyden jar in 1752 for his famous experiments with lightning. He attached a key to a silk ribbon that was tied to a kite and flew the kite during a thunderstorm. Fortunately, Franklin's kite wasn't hit by lightning (he wouldn't have lived to finish the experiment if it had been), but he did draw a negative charge from charged water vapor and particles in the air. The charge traveled down the kite ribbon and collected in a Leyden jar that Franklin had attached to the lower end of the ribbon.

We still have a need for storing electrical charge. The modern name for a device like the Leyden jar, which stores electricity through a separation of opposite charges, is a *capacitor*. You'll find capacitors in electronic devices, such as a computer, which can continue to store information even when the power is off.

Some people give credit for the invention of the Leyden jar to a German cleric named Ewald Georg von Kleist. About the same time Musschenbroek's device shocked Cunaeus, Kleist shocked himself performing a nearly identical experiment. Because Musschenbroek investigated the accident more thoroughly and went on to develop an effective device for storing electricity, the device was named in Musschenbroek's honor for his native city.

INVENTOR'S CHALLENGE

Can you invent a device that will let you know whether your Leyden jar is charged?

Materials

glass or plastic jar
piece of wooden dowel longer than the width of the jar
aluminum foil
scissors

CLUES

Remember that objects with an identical charge repel one another.

21 Battery

The Problem

It is about 1791, and you are a physics professor at the University of Pavia in Italy. You have been experimenting with static electricity for many years and are quite excited to receive a copy of a paper written by your good friend Luigi Galvani, a professor of medicine. Galvani has written about a series of experiments with dissected frogs' legs, which he has undertaken in the past several years. Most interesting to you is Galvani's discovery that a dead frog's legs twitched when he held a copper wire in one hand, an iron bar in the other, and then touched the copper and iron to the frog's legs.

Galvani's research leads him to conclude that animals, dead or alive, possess "animal electricity." You think something else is involved—but what?

Observation

You have discovered that if you join a piece of copper and a piece of zinc into a V-shape and then stick your tongue into the V, you get an odd, bitter taste. When you separate the two pieces of metal, the taste disappears.

MATERIALS

Experiment A
  6-inch (15-cm) piece of copper wire
  zinc-coated (*galvanized*) nail
  lemon or lemon juice
  small bowl

Experiment B
  lemon juice and bowl from Experiment A
  paper towel
  scissors
  20 pennies
  20 dimes

Experiment A

1. Pick up the nail with one hand and the copper wire with the other. Touch the nail and the wire to your tongue. What does it taste like?

2. Squeeze or pour the lemon juice into a small dish.

3. Dip one end of the nail and one end of the copper wire in the lemon juice. Keeping the ends in the lemon juice, touch the other ends to your tongue. Taste something different? You should feel a tingle or a funny taste where the nail touches your tongue.

Experiment B

1. Cut the paper towel into nineteen 1- × 1-inch (2.5- × 2.5-cm) squares, and soak them in the dish of lemon juice.

2. Make a column of the coins and the paper towel squares by first putting a penny, then a square of paper towel, then a dime, then a

square of towel, then a penny, and so on. Wet your hand and place the column in your palm. Touch your tongue to the top coin, as shown. Did you get a tingle? You've made a wet-cell battery!

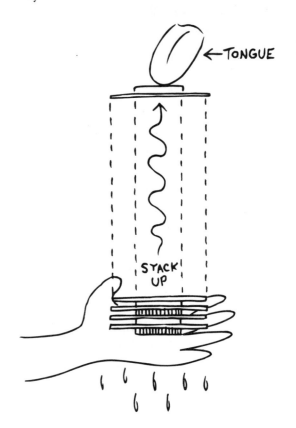

As you saw in the comb experiment in Chapter 20, you can use friction to strip the electrons from the atoms in one material and transfer them to another material. When you rubbed the comb with the cloth, the comb became negatively charged and the cloth became positively charged.

In this experiment, the lemon juice, which is an acid, chemically strips electrons from atoms in the copper. The freed electrons from the copper then flow toward the zinc in the nail, which attracts them. When you touch your tongue to the copper and zinc, you create an electrical circuit that runs from the copper wire through your tongue to the zinc-coated nail and back through the lemon juice to the copper wire. You feel the flow of electrons as a tingle and an odd taste.

Galvani did much the same thing when he experimented with copper and iron touching the frog's legs. Acids built up in the dead frog. Those acids chemically stripped electrons from the copper, and those electrons then flowed toward the iron. Instead of a tingle or a taste, the electricity affected the frog's muscles and made them twitch.

When you stacked the coins and the lemon-juice-soaked paper-towel squares, you created 10 chemical reactions that stripped electrons from the copper pennies and added them to the zinc in the dimes. When you touched your tongue to the stack, the electrons moved through your body and back to the stack through your hand. The larger the stack of coins, the greater the number of electrons moving, and the greater the flow of electricity, or *voltage*.

Answers from the Past

Professor of medicine Luigi Galvani often used dissected frogs in his experiments. During the late 1780s, he observed that a dead frog's legs twitched when they were touched with the current from a static-electricity generator or from a charged Leyden jar (see Chapter 20). He also found that the legs sometimes twitched when there was no electrical charge nearby. He hung the legs on an iron railing with a copper hook and was surprised to find the legs twitching away.

Galvani concluded that animals possessed a special electrical property that was part of the animal, alive or dead. He called this property "animal electricity." He wrote his results and his hypothesis in a pamphlet and sent it to other scientists, including his friend and fellow professor, Alessandro Volta.

Volta doubted that animal electricity was the explanation for the odd behavior of the frog's legs. He thought it had something to do with the metals that touched the frog. To gather more information, he made a V out of copper and zinc pieces and put his tongue into the V. He got a peculiar taste. Volta eventually hypothesized that the metal strips not only conducted electricity, but also, along with his saliva, created it.

In 1797, Volta tried a new experiment. He made a column or "pile" of 10 pairs of silver and zinc plates. Each pair was separated by a piece of wet cloth. When he put one hand on the bottom of the pile of 20 plates and the other on the top, he could feel the tingle of electricity. As long as the pieces of cloth remained wet, the pile produced electricity. This was the world's first battery—called a *voltaic pile*, named after its inventor—that produced a continuous flow of electricity! Volta soon found that if he used copper instead of silver and an acid instead of water, he could produce more electricity. Within a few years, scientists were making batteries with thousands of metal plates!

The word *voltage* means the energy carried by charges that make up a current. Alessandro Volta's name was used to acknowledge his contribution to advancing the understanding of electricity.

The batteries we use today in flashlights and toys are called dry-cell batteries. They work much the same way Volta's batteries did. Inside a dry-cell battery are two different substances, usually carbon and zinc, in contact with a strong acid. The acid slowly dissolves the zinc, leaving electrons behind in the zinc, which becomes negatively charged. One end of the battery has an *electrode* (a piece of metal that conducts electricity and sticks out of the battery) in the zinc, and the other end has an electrode in the carbon. When a wire connects the two ends, electrons flow from one electrode, through the wire, and through the other electrode, and then back to the first. Electricity flows until the chemical reaction comes to an end.

INVENTOR'S CHALLENGE

Can you make a battery out of fruits or vegetables?

Materials

> potato
> lemon
> apple
> penny
> dime
> insulated copper wire
> voltmeter

CLUES

Use a voltmeter to discover which makes the highest voltage battery. Can you make a stronger battery by linking several fruits or vegetables together?

[22] Electric Generator

The Problem

It's 1831, and you are an English chemist. You have worked for 10 years investigating magnetism and electricity, reading everything you can about the two subjects. You have even written a book summarizing scientists' progress to date. You are convinced that it is possible to create electricity from magnets. Other scientists have been trying to do so for 20 years, and most have given up on the idea, but you are convinced there is a way. . . .

Observations

For your chemistry experiments in your lab, you use electricity generated by *voltaic piles,* the batteries invented by Alessandro Volta in 1797 (see Chapter 21). Using a voltaic pile, you've repeated an experiment first demonstrated by Danish scientist Hans Ørsted in 1820, in which a wire carrying electrical current is shown to act as a magnet. The electricity created a magnetic field around the wire.

You reason that if electricity can create a magnetic force, then you should be able to use magnets to create electricity. . . .

MATERIALS

adult helper
one 6-foot (180-cm) piece and one 4-foot
  (120-cm) piece of insulated copper wire
wire stripper
empty, clean 12-oz (355-ml) plastic soda bottle
scissors
duct tape
wooden table to work on
small, inexpensive compass
empty toilet-paper tube
modeling clay
6-inch (15-cm) bar magnet

Experiment

1. Ask your adult helper to strip about 4
inches (10 cm) of the insulation off both ends
of both wires.

2. Ask your adult helper to cut a 3-inch
(7.5-cm) section out of the middle of the
plastic soda bottle. Wrap a bunch of the longer
piece of wire around and around this middle
section of the soda bottle, as shown. Leave
about 12 inches (30 cm) of wire at both ends.
Use the duct tape to secure the coil of wire to
the plastic. Put the plastic piece on its side, and
rest the compass inside. Adjust the plastic piece
so that the compass needle points north and
lines up with the coil, as shown.

3. Wrap the shorter piece of wire around the
length of the toilet paper roll in a neat spiral, as
shown. The coils shouldn't touch one another.
Leave about 12 inches (30 cm) of wire at both
ends. Set the toilet paper roll on its end. You
may need to stick it in some modeling clay to
make it stable.

4. Twist the ends of the bare wire sticking
out from the toilet-paper roll to the ends of
the bare wire sticking out from the soda bottle.
Make sure the two twisted connections don't
touch each other.

5. Dip one end of the magnet in and out of
the toilet paper roll. Watch what happens to
the compass needle. (You may need a partner
to watch the needle while you move the magnet.) The movement of the compass needle
signals that you have generated electricity! You
have created an electrical generator!

The compass needle will move slightly as
you move the magnet in and out of the
coil of wire. It moves because the movement of the magnet generates electricity.
The electricity flowing through the wire
magnetizes the wire. It creates a magnetic
field around it. That magnetic field is what
deflects the compass needle.

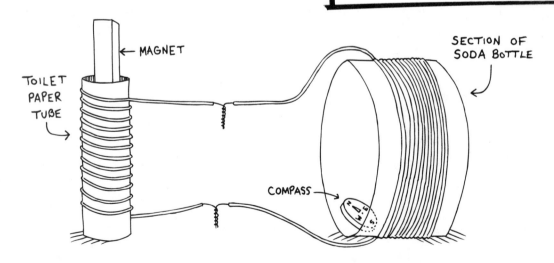

Answers from the Past

Michael Faraday was born in England in 1791. His father, a blacksmith, was often sick and could barely provide food and housing, much less an education, for his three children. Michael, the middle child, had only one year of schooling, but he always had a great love of learning. As a 13-year-old, he was apprenticed to a bookbinder to learn the trade of making books, and he used the opportunity to read the many books about science that passed through his master's shop. Then one lucky day in 1812, he was given a ticket to hear famous English chemist Humphry Davy give a series of lectures. Young Faraday took notes on the lectures, bound the notes into a book, gave the book to Davy, and then asked if he could be an assistant in Davy's lab at the Royal Institution in London. Davy agreed to hire him.

Working with Davy, Faraday became intrigued by magnets and electricity. Over the preceding decades, many scientists had been investigating the nature of electricity. One of the most significant findings was made by a Danish physicist, Hans Christian Ørsted. While demonstrating how electricity flowed from a battery through a wire, Ørsted accidentally discovered that a nearby compass needle moved. He experimented further and found that a cylindrical magnetic field is generated around a wire when the wire is electrified.

Ørsted's experiment inspired Faraday. He immediately suspected that if electricity could generate magnetism, then magnetism should generate electricity. Many scientists had also thought of this possibility, but none had been able to make it work. The famous French scientist André-Marie Ampère, who worked out some of the fundamental laws of electricity and magnetism, even announced in 1825 that it was impossible to *induce* (to bring forth or generate) electricity from magnets.

Faraday struggled with the problem for years. He carried a bar magnet and a length of copper wire in his pocket so he could work on the problem in any spare moment. He tried all sorts of configurations of copper wire and magnet to see whether he could generate an electrical current that he could detect by making a compass needle move. He worked for 10 years without success.

Then, one day in 1831, as he disconnected an electrical circuit made of a battery and bare copper wire, Faraday noticed the needle in a compass nearby seemed to flicker. He experimented some more and began to see that that production of electricity required more than wrapping a copper wire around a magnet. Electricity

---

Ørsted went further with his discovery. He twisted a wire so that it formed a coil. When he ran electrical current through the coil (called a **solenoid**) by attaching the ends of the wire to the ends of a battery, he discovered that each loop produced a magnetic field. He also found that each loop added to the total strength of the magnetic field produced by the coil. A solenoid produced a strong magnetic field at both ends and in the center of the coil.

In 1825, an English experimenter, William Sturgeon, discovered that when the coils of a solenoid are wrapped around a piece of iron, it becomes an **electromagnet**. The solenoid magnetizes the iron, and the strength of the magnetic field of the iron is added to the solenoid's magnetic force. An electromagnet can be designed to lift objects thousands of times its own weight.

was generated only when a magnetic field was interrupted. On October 17, 1831, Faraday put together a combination of wires, a magnet, and a compass similar to the one that you made, and he got the same result that you did. The key to making electricity is moving the magnet in and out of the copper coil.

Faraday quickly went on to create larger generators. He called his electricity machines *dynamos,* machines that produce *dynamic* (continuous) power.

INVENTOR'S CHALLENGE

Make the strongest electromagnet you can, using no more than three 1.5-volt batteries. What two factors, other than the voltage of the battery, affect the power of an electromagnet?

Materials

iron nails or other rod-shaped pieces of iron or steel
insulated copper wire
wire stripper
three 1.5-volt batteries
tape
iron or steel objects to pick up
adult helper

CLUES

After you've prepared your electromagnet, tape one stripped end of the copper wire to either end of the chain of batteries. Don't leave your battery connected for long: Its power drains quickly.

[23] Electric Motor

The Problem

It is 1833. You are Thomas Davenport, a poor, self-educated blacksmith in Brandon, Vermont, who has become utterly fascinated by the recently invented electromagnet. You are convinced that it is possible to produce mechanical motion using these powerful new devices. You and your brother, a peddler, have just sold your brother's wares, as well as your horse, to buy a large electromagnet. With your wife, you have taken apart the magnet, learned how it is made, and made two more of your own. Now, you are ready to try to produce mechanical power from electricity . . . but how?

Observations

Just last year, at the Penfield and Hammond Iron Works at Crown Point across Lake Champlain from your town, a wonderful new process using electromagnets was announced. Engineers at the Iron Works used electromagnets to magnetize iron spikes attached to a rotating wooden barrel. As the barrel turns and crushed rock passes under it, the spikes attract the valuable iron ore, separating it from the useless rubble. You made the 25-mile (40-km) trip to Crown Point on horseback to see just how the invention worked.

Inspired by this display of the power of electromagnetism, you read as much as you can find about the subject. You now understand how Michael Faraday induced a flow of electricity in a copper coil by continuously moving a magnet in and out of the coil. You are sure that if mechanical movement can generate electricity, then electricity can generate mechanical movement. You decide to experiment with arrangements of batteries, copper wire, and magnets.

MATERIALS

26-gauge magnet wire with colored *enamel* insulation (available at a home-electronics store)

toilet-paper tube

scissors

fine sandpaper

newspaper or cardboard

two uncoated jumbo paper clips

adult helper or needle-nosed pliers

wide rubber band

fresh 1.5-volt (D-cell) alkaline battery

rectangular ceramic magnet (available at a home-electronics store)

Experiment

1. Leaving about a 3-inch (8-cm) tail, wrap the wire around the toilet-paper tube seven times, as shown. (Make the seven loops in a single circle, not a spiral.) Remove the tube. Cut the wire, leaving another 3-inch (8-cm) tail. The tails should stick out from the loop *directly opposite* each other. Wrap each tail around the loop so that the loop is held together and so that the tails are perpendicular to the loop, as shown.

2. Use the sandpaper to remove all the insulation from one tail, except for about ⅛ inch (3 mm) of the insulation on the tail where it meets the loop. The tail should be shiny copper.

3. Put the coil down flat on a table (put a section of newspaper or cardboard underneath to protect the table). Sand off the insulation from only the top surface of the other tail. Leave about ⅛ inch (3 mm) of full insulation on this tail where it meets the loop. This tail should be shiny copper on one side and colored on the other.

4. Bend both of the paper clips into a V shape, as shown. (You may need to have an adult helper do this, or you may need to use a needle-nosed pliers.)

5. Fit the rubber band around the battery to cover the terminals at the ends. The rubber band should be snug, so you may have to loop it twice.

6. Slip the large end of each paper clip under the rubber band at each end, so that the paper clips make contact with the terminals, as shown. The paper clips must be positioned parallel to each other.

7. Stick the ceramic magnet to the side of the battery so that it is parallel to the battery, as shown. Hold the battery in the middle with one hand. Rest the tails of the wire loop in the cradle formed by the ends of the paper clips sticking out from the battery, as shown. (Make sure that the tails do not rest on their small, unsanded portions.)

TAIL
WRAP 7 TIMES
TAIL

BENT PAPER CLIP

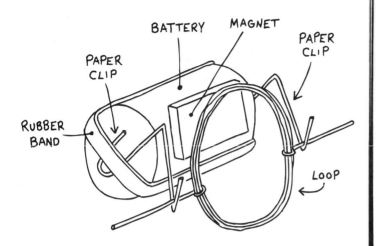

PAPER CLIP

BATTERY

MAGNET

PAPER CLIP

PAPER CLIP

RUBBER BAND

LOOP

8. Give the loop a little push. The loop should spin rapidly. You've made a direct-current (DC) motor, similar in principle to the one Thomas Davenport made in 1833.

Note: If the loop doesn't spin at first, make sure the paper clips are exactly parallel and that they make contact with the sanded portions of the tails. Try turning the battery so that the magnet is in a slightly different position relative to the loop.

Answers from the Past

Thomas Davenport was born on a farm in 1802, the eighth of 12 children. His father died when he was 10 years old, and at age 14, Thomas was indentured for seven years to a blacksmith. He never got the formal education he wanted (his master was required to send him to school for only six weeks per year), but the boy was a great reader and full of curiosity.

As a blacksmith in the village of Brandon, Vermont, he heard about the developments at the nearby Penfield and Hammond Iron Works. Penfield and Hammond was the first company to harness electricity as an essential part of its

How does this motor work? Electricity flows from the battery through the uninsulated copper tails and the wire loop, which then become an electromagnet. One face of the coil becomes a north pole, the other a south pole. The magnet attached to the battery attracts its opposite pole on the coil and repels its like pole, causing the coil to turn.

When the loop turns to face the magnet, the insulation you left on one surface of one tail comes into contact with the paper clip so that the current stops flowing. The loop is now no longer an electromagnet and is no longer attracted to the magnet. Inertia causes the loop to continue on its turning path. When the loop completes half a turn, the uninsulated side of the tail contacts the paper clip again, and current flows again. The loop is once again attracted to the magnet, and the cycle repeats.

business. Davenport, by then 30 years old, was fascinated by the magnetic ore separator and by the new electromagnets that made it work.

Poor as he was, Davenport was determined to have an electromagnet. His brother, who pitched in to help him buy a large one, thought they ought to exhibit the electromagnet and charge a fee for viewing it, but Thomas had other ideas. After he and his wife, Emily, figured out how the electromagnet worked, he built two of his own. (Emily insulated the wire with strips of cloth from her wedding dress.) He powered the electromagnets with homemade chemical batteries (see Chapter 21 on the early battery) and then experimented until he arranged them so they would generate motion.

Davenport's motor was similar to the one you made. He fixed one magnet to a horizontal wheel. He fixed another to a stationary frame. The magnet on the wheel, attracted to the stationary magnet, moved toward it, turning the wheel half a rotation. At first, to complete the turn, Davenport reversed the wires to one of the magnets, which reversed the poles of the magnet so that it pushed the wheel away. Later he made a device (called a *brush and commutator*) that automatically reversed the poles of the electromagnet on the wheel, so that the wheel would turn continuously.

Davenport could have used his motor to drive some of the equipment in his blacksmith's shop. Instead, he devoted his energy to developing his electric motor as a safer engine for locomotives. (Boiler explosions in steam-driven locomotive engines were frequent and often tragic occurrences at the time.) In 1837, the motor he designed received the first patent not only for an electric motor, but also for any electric machine.

Davenport's motor was a great technological success, but he never earned any money from it. The problem was that the power in chemical batteries was unpredictable. Steam engines, which burn wood or coal to boil water, provided more reliable power than motors powered by chemical batteries. It was not until the 1880s, when electricity was being centrally produced (by water-powered or steam-powered generators) and distributed over wires, that electric motors would become a success. Unfortunately, Davenport died, bankrupt and frustrated, in 1851, and he never knew how the electric motor changed the world.

INVENTOR'S CHALLENGE

Can you think of a way to make your motor perform work?

CLUE

You can bend the free ends of the wire tails, but make sure they're bent in opposite directions.

[24] Telegraph

The Problem

It is 1836. You are Samuel Morse, a 41-year-old American artist who specializes in painting portraits. You also have a curious mind that is drawn to solving technological puzzles. Four years ago, at dinner on a ship carrying you home from Europe, a fellow voyager intrigued you with demonstrations of electricity using batteries, wires, and magnets. People, he noted, were coming to believe that electricity can pass through any length of wire instantaneously. At that moment, you became fascinated with using electricity as a way to transmit information over long distances. Wouldn't it be wonderful if you could use electricity to send messages to another part of the world in an instant!

Observations

You know that in 1746, a French scientist demonstrated that a burst of static electricity could travel at least a mile through a wire. You also know that in 1831, American scientist Joseph Henry was able to overcome the tendency for the force of an electrical current to decline over long stretches of wire by arranging batteries in a series.

I n 1746, a French abbé named Jean-Antoine Nollet arranged for about 200 monks to stand in a long row, each one 25 feet (7.5 meters) away from the next. Each monk held the end of a 25-foot piece of iron wire in either hand, so that all of them were connected by wire to each other. Suddenly, the abbé touched the first monk in the row with a strong static electricity spark. The entire mile-long row of white-robed monks leaped in the air simultaneously!

Telegraph systems based on visual signs are widespread in Europe at this time. Signalmen stationed in hilltop towers arrange huge bars or colored panels in patterns that can be seen from a tower miles away. The patterns are decoded as letters or words. Each signalman passes the signal along to the next tower.

MATERIALS

18 inches (45 cm) of insulated wire
adult helper
wire stripper
metal thumbtack
piece of corrugated cardboard or Styrofoam
electrical tape
D-cell battery
1.5-volt bulb with bulb holder (available from a consumer-electronics store)
metal key

Experiment

1. Cut three pieces of wire about 6 inches (15 cm) long each. Ask an adult helper to use a wire stripper to strip off about 1 inch (2.5 cm) of insulation from both ends of each piece of wire.

2. Twist the end of one wire around one thumbtack. Push the tack firmly into the cardboard or Styrofoam.

3. Use tape to attach the other end of the wire to one end of the battery.

4. Tape the end of a second wire to the other end of the battery.

5. Attach the other end of the second wire to one side of the bulb holder.

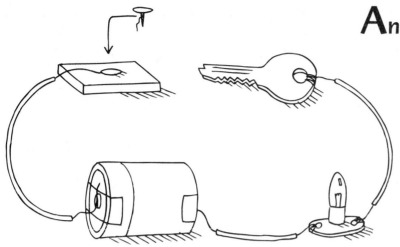

6. Attach one end of the third wire to the other side of the bulb holder. Attach the other end of the third wire to the key.

7. Make sure the contacts between all metal parts are secure.

8. Touch the key to the thumbtack. The bulb should light up because you've completed an electric circuit. If it doesn't, reconnect the wires to make sure there's good contact between the wire and the tack, the bulb holder, and the battery.

> In this electrical circuit, electricity flows from one end of the battery through conducting materials and back to the other end of the battery. Metals and the bulb holder are good conductors of electricity.

9. Break the circuit by lifting the key. The light will go off. Now, use the key to make the bulb flash quickly three times, then flash more slowly three times, then flash quickly again three times. You've sent the international telegraphic signal for "Help!" You've tapped the Morse code for the letters "S-O-S" (which stands for "Save Our Ship!").

Answers from the Past

For thousands of years, people all over the world have needed to communicate with each other over a distance. Native Americans used smoke signals during the day (and shot up flaming arrows at night) to communicate simple messages to people miles away. African tribes used a pattern of drumbeats passed on from tribe to tribe to talk to others out of sight. When people needed to communicate over longer distances or needed to send a complex or private message, they sent a messenger. The message traveled at about 4 miles (6.4 km) per hour, the speed of a person on foot. After the horse was domesticated in about 3000 B.C., the message could go faster—up to 10 miles (16 km) per hour. Even the fastest sailing ships delivered messages across water at about the speed of a horse.

Until the 1790s, the world had seen no real improvement in the speed of communications. In 1791, however, two French brothers, René and Claude Chappe, pioneered a new system for sending messages over distances. Their first *télégraphe* (meaning "far writer") was a large, pivoting wooden panel placed on top of a castle. One side of the panel was painted white and the other black. By using a code book and flipping the panel from one side to the other in a pattern, René composed and sent a message. At a house 10 miles (16 km) away, Claude, using a telescope to view the panel and another copy of the code book, translated the series of flashes of black and white. A message had traveled 10 miles (16 km) in four minutes, 15 times the speed of a horse.

Within a few years, many of the governments of Europe were building a variety of optical telegraph systems using a series of hilltop towers. By the 1830s—when Morse was painting in Europe—the optical telegraph created links between such distant countries as France, Russia, Italy, and Finland. The system was effective only during daylight and in good weather, but it changed the way people thought about time and distance.

> **T**he optical telegraph was used primarily within a country so that a military commander could alert political leaders in the capital about dangers at the borders. Napoleon, however, saw another possibility in the new invention. He approved the idea of sending the winning lottery numbers (drawn in Paris) throughout France by optical telegraph. This action ended fraud in the national lottery. Cheaters were no longer able to learn the lottery results in Paris and then ride to smaller towns to place bets before the official lottery results arrived days later by mail coach.

Samuel F. B. Morse, an excellent American painter, was also a creative problem solver. (When he was 26 years old, he invented a new water pump for firefighting.) He started working on the electric telegraph in 1832, with no knowledge of electricity. While Morse imagined that electrical pulses could replace the visual signs of the optical telegraph, he didn't have the electrical expertise he needed to fulfill his vision. He relied heavily on the work and advice of scientists such as Joseph Henry to make a practical system for conveying electrical current over long distances. He also relied on the mechanical expertise of his partner, Alfred Vail, to design and construct the sending and receiving devices.

Morse did invent a unique and efficient telegraph code. Shorter and longer electrical pulses created a series of dots and dashes, which corresponded to the letters of the alphabet. Other inventors, such as Charles Wheatstone and William Cooke in England, developed an electrical telegraph, too, but their systems relied on multiple wires, dials, and complex code books. The simplicity of Morse's system won out.

In 1844, the first American electric telegraph line was established among Baltimore, Maryland, and Washington, D.C., a distance of about 50 miles (80 km). By 1852, there were more than 23,000 (36,000 km) miles of commercial telegraph line in the United States. Soon, with the laying of undersea telegraph cables, there was no obstacle to nearly instantaneous worldwide communication.

> **T**o send the electrical signals, Morse used a metal lever (instead of the key you used) to complete an electrical circuit. He created two different signals. One he produced with a quick tap of the lever, quickly completing and then breaking the circuit. He produced a second type of signal by holding down the lever a little longer, so that the electrical circuit remained for a little longer before it was disrupted.
>
> Morse's partner, Alfred Vail, invented a receiving device to make the electrical signals understandable to the person at the other end of the wire. The device had a long strip of paper that moved at a steady rate and a pen poised above it. When the circuit was completed at the sending end and a signal arrived, the pen hit the paper. When the sender broke the circuit and the signal ended, the pen lifted. A short signal made the pen produce a dot. The longer signal held the pen down longer, so it produced a dash on the paper. (Morse couldn't use a lightbulb as you did, of course, because Edison wouldn't invent the lightbulb until 1880.)

Morse wanted his code to be as efficient as possible. He figured out which letters were used most often in English by counting the number of pieces of type for each letter in a printer's type tray. He represented "E" with the fastest signal to send—one dot—because it is the most frequently used letter in the English alphabet. Here is the code he developed:

A ·–	J ·———	S ···	2 ··———
B –···	K –·–	T –	3 ···——
C –·–·	L ·–··	U ··–	4 ····—
D –··	M ——	V ···—	5 ·····
E ·	N –·	W ·——	6 –····
F ··–·	O ———	X –··–	7 ——···
G ——·	P ·——·	Y –·——	8 ———··
H ····	Q ——·–	Z ——··	9 ————·
I ··	R ·–·	1 ·————	0 —————

INVENTOR'S CHALLENGE

In 1792, the Chappe brothers developed a new optical telegraph that looked like a person with his arms outstretched. The arms of their telegraph could pivot at the shoulder and could bend up and down at the elbow. Can you reinvent their optical telegraph and create a code book for 26 letters and 10 numbers? Make two telegraphs, and "talk" silently with a friend.

Materials

modeling clay
corrugated cardboard
scissors
nail
brass brad paper fasteners (the kind with a head and two legs that can be bent)

Glossary

absolute zero: the temperature at which the molecules of a substance would theoretically stop moving; -273° C or -460° F.

air pressure: the weight of air.

anemometer: a device for measuring the speed of wind.

aneroid: using no fluid.

archaeologist: a person who studies past human cultures by studying tools, pottery, and other relics of the past.

axle: a bar on which one or more wheels turn.

balance: a device for measuring the weight of objects, typically consisting of a bar with a fulcrum in the center and pans at either end.

barometer: a device for measuring air pressure.

bilge: the empty space far below the deck of a ship, where water collects.

binder: a substance that causes the pigments in a paint to stick to each other.

block and tackle: a set of pulleys and the cord running through them, which can be used to lift objects.

carbohydrate: a compound, such as sugar or starch, that is composed of carbon, hydrogen, and oxygen.

casein: a protein in milk.

catapult: an ancient war machine that launched stones or other objects from the end of a long scoop attached to, and powered by, a twisted cord or other fibers.

Celsius scale: a temperature scale in which 0° is the melting point of fresh water and 100° is the boiling point of fresh water.

centrifugal force: a force that causes objects moving in a circle to move outward from the center of the circle.

chaff: husks of grains such as wheat.

conductor: a substance or device that readily permits electricity, heat, or sound to pass through it.

contract: to become smaller.

counterweight trebuchet: a medieval war machine that launched stones or other objects, consisting of a long scoop balanced on a tall fulcrum; the ammunition in the bowl of the scoop was launched by the release of heavy objects on the opposite end.

crossbow: a weapon made of a flexible material held parallel to the ground, the ends of which are pulled into a curved shape by a cord or other fiber; a trigger releases the rope, which launches a stone, arrow, or other object.

cup anemometer: a device for measuring the wind's speed, based on the rotation of cups around a vertical axis.

direct dye: a substance that colors materials without using a mordant.

dye: a substance used to change the color of something

dyebath: mixture of hot water and dye.

egg tempera: a paint made by mixing egg yolk and water.

electric field: field around charged particles, which exerts a force on other charged particles.

electromagnet: a device consisting of an iron or steel core, magnetized by electrical current in a coil that surrounds it.

electron: a subatomic particle with a negative charge.

equilateral: having all the sides equal in length.

Fahrenheit scale: a temperature scale in which 0° is the freezing temperature of salt water, 32° is the freezing point of fresh water, and 212° is the boiling point of fresh water.

fixed pulley: a rope or belt wrapped around a wheel that is attached to a structure and therefore provides no mechanical advantage, but that does change the direction of the force required to lift an object.

fluorescent: capable of emitting light.

friction: the resistance between two objects when they are pushed or pulled across one another.

fulcrum: the point on which a lever turns or is supported when it is moving or lifting something.

gall: a bump on oak trees, caused by certain flies or wasps.

geodesic dome: a domelike structure made from triangular pieces of a light material, such as plastic, joined together.

grounding: the process of connecting an electrical circuit or charge to Earth.

hypothesis: a possible explanation of a set of facts.

icosahedron: a geometric solid made of 20 equilateral triangles.

igloo: a dome-shaped Inuit house built out of hard snow.

inclined plane: a flat, slanted surface

indirect dye: a substance that requires a mordant to permanently color a material.

induction by grounding: a method of giving an electrical charge to an object by drawing its electrons to Earth.

inertia: the property of matter that tends to resist any change in rate of motion or in rest.

insulation: a substance that minimizes the leakage of heat, electricity, or sound.

insulation: a material that does not allow an electrical charge to flow freely.

Kelvin scale: a temperature scale in which 0° is absolute zero.

kiln: a special, high-temperature oven used to heat and harden pottery, among other uses.

kinetic energy: the energy of motion.

lever: a bar that tilts on a fulcrum.

lodestone: a variety of magnetite, a common black mineral that acts as a magnet.

mechanical advantage: the number of times that a machine multiplies the effort of the user of the machine.

mechanics: the branch of physics that deals with the effect of forces on things.

mordant: a chemical substance used in dyeing to make a color permanent.

moveable pulley: a pulley that is not attached to a structure and therefore provides a mechanical advantage to the user.

neutron: a subatomic particle with no charge.

papyrus: a material made of the stems and inner core of the papyrus plant and used for writing on.

parchment: a sheep or goat skin specially prepared to use as a writing surface.

pentagon: five-sided figure.

photosynthesis: the process by which green plants use sunlight, water, and carbon dioxide to produce food.

pigment: a dry substance that doesn't dissolve in water, but that can be mixed in another liquid to become a paint or ink.

pivot: an object on or around which another object turns.

pole: either of two ends of a magnetic material.

potential energy: possible or stored energy that can become kinetic energy.

proton: a subatomic particle with a positive charge.

pyrometric: capable of measuring high temperatures by means of physical change.

scientific method: method of research that involves taking precise measurements, making repeated experiments to test a hypothesis, and drawing logical conclusions from data.

scribe: a person who copies manuscripts as a profession.

shadoof: a device used for lifting water, consisting of a long rod suspended horizontally on a fulcrum with a bucket at one end and a weight at the other.

simple machines: a group of machines that includes the inclined plane, the wedge, the screw, the lever, the pulley, and the wheel and axle.

slurry: a mixture of water and a substance that doesn't dissolve in water.

socket: an opening or hollow that forms a holder for something else.

solenoid: a coil-shaped wire carrying current, which has magnetic properties.

static electricity: an electrical charge that is stationary and does not flow from the charged object.

tension: the act of stretching or the condition of being stretched.

textiles: cloth or goods made from woven strands of fibers of plant material, animal hair, or other materials.

thermometer: a device that measures heat.

thermoscope: a device that detects heat but doesn't measure it.

tipi: a Native American dwelling made of long poles arranged in a conical shape and covered with animal hides.

torsion: twisting.

traction trebuchet: a medieval war machine that launched stones or other objects; consisted of a long scoop balanced on a tall fulcrum; the ammunition in the bowl of the scoop was launched when soldiers pulled down the end opposite the bowl.

trajectory: a curved path of an object in flight.

trapezoid: a four-sided figure that has two parallel and two nonparallel sides.

travois: a device for transport, using two long poles and a wide sling.

vacuum: a space that is empty of matter.

vertices: plural of vertex, the intersection of two sides of a plane (flat) figure.

wash: a mixture of pigment and a liquid, which can be used for painting.

wheel and axle: a simple machine made up of two cylindrical objects of different sizes; a force is applied to the wheel and transferred to the axle.

wigwam: a round- or oval-shaped Native American dwelling made from many wood poles, covered in bark or reed mats.

wind vane: a device that indicates the wind's direction.

winnow: to free grain from the lighter particles of chaff by throwing the chaff and grain into the air and letting the wind blow away the chaff.

Index